THE

$\mathscr{B}$EAUTY

OF

$\mathscr{H}$OLINESS

MASHANI ALLEN

Cover Design: MaShani Allen
Author Photo: J'Nae Antoinette Photography
The Beauty of Holiness: A Practical Guide to Life, Relationships & Inner Beauty
Visit the author's website at www.MaShaniAllen.com

Library of Congress Cataloging-in-Publication Data:
An application to register this book for cataloging has been submitted to the Library of Congress.

International Standard Book Number:
ISBN-10: 1682732398
ISBN-13: 9781682732397

Second edition
Printed in the United States of America

Connect with MaShani and join her mailing list at www.MaShaniAllen.com

Dedication

This book is dedicated to all the women who went before me, those who stand with me and those who will come after me.

This book by MaShani Allen is inspired in due season. The timing of such a treasure is immeasurable in its importance to the body of Christ. The information provided is for "such a time as this" to help all of us to be better prepared for the coming of our Lord and Savior Jesus Christ for his church.

I know the author to be truly dedicated and a sincere person in Christ. It has certainly been both a pleasure and a privilege to have mentored the author of this great work. I am grateful to God for whatever degree of influence my wife and I have had on her life and her spiritual development. To God be the glory!

May God continue to bless and prosper her in all her endeavors and her service to the body of Christ.

Dr. Gilbert S. Smith
Pastor, Apostolic Revival Center

Every woman reading this book will be profoundly impacted to be all that God has intended for her. With insight, revelation and strategy to apply to life in a practical way this book is a must read for all.

Knowing MaShani personally as Pastor and friend, she is genuine, modeling the truth written in her book. As a woman of righteousness and integrity she is one who not only teaches but also lives out her convictions written.

Dr. Cathy Guerrero
Pastor, Regency Christian Center Int'l
Founder/CEO Life Builder Seminars

Foreword

When I was the tender and awkward age of twelve I was a tomboy who was just discovering that I really wanted to be pretty. I was standing at the bus stop at school one day when a teenage girl said to me "You are either a cute boy or an ugly girl. Which are you?" I was embarrassed ....no, horrified.... that she could not tell if I was a boy or a girl! Until that time, my outward appearance didn't really matter that much to me, however, suddenly as I was approaching my teen years I began to notice how beautiful some of my classmates had grown to be. I longed to be someone others might notice. Though I began to work hard on my appearance, it wasn't until I received Jesus as my Savior at the age of fourteen that my real makeover began. I found such a place in His love that gave me confidence and courage to be who I was called to be. Beauty, for me, began on the inside and worked its way out.

Yet we hear the cry of so many women saying, "I am not thin enough!" "I am not tall enough!" "I hate my nose!" "If I only looked more like her, people would notice me." We live in a world in which airbrushed pictures in magazines create an unrealistic idea of what beauty really is causing many women to see themselves less lovely than they truly are.

God's Word encourages us that it is not wise nor healthy to compare ourselves to one another, yet many women spend their lives, not to mention a great deal of money, striving to fit an ideal that only exists in their minds. This insecurity can often set women up to form unhealthy self-images which lead to unhealthy relationships with other women and especially men. All the while the Lord is longing to draw us to His heart, to whisper words of love, to let us know just how beautiful we can be, inside and out, as our lives are filled with His glory and the beauty of His holiness.

True beauty cannot be judged by merely looking at someone's outward appearance. True beauty is that which resonates from within, lighting one's countenance, lifting one's soul. A woman finds true beauty as she looks into the eyes of her Maker, her Beloved, and finds a place of unconditional love and acceptance. This love brings healing to the soul and the courage to shine as God intended.

This delightful book by MaShani Allen will encourage and strengthen you to identify spiritual "beauty treatments" that will set you free. These "beauty tips" will release you to a deeper love relationship with Him, healthier relationships with others and a kindness towards yourself that will increase your level of peace and joy in life. Yes, you were created to sparkle and shine as the beauty of holiness pours out of your life.

Jane Hamon
Vision Church @Christian International
Senior Co-Pastor

Introduction

Being Apostolic means we believe in the teaching of the apostles and prophets. Jesus Christ himself being the chief cornerstone. The apostolic woman believes, teaches and lives this according to the word of God. She should be an example of the standards of the church of our Lord Jesus Christ. All women should be able to look at her and see a pattern that they can follow. She is obedient to the word of God and she is willing to assist in the service of God wherever she is needed. She holds a high spiritual and social position in the Kingdom of God. She is polite, refined, well-mannered and above all she is chosen by God for salvation and eternal life. Walk in the Beauty of Holiness. Talk in the Beauty of Holiness. - *Althea Allen*

Those are the words of my grandmother, written decades before my reading them. This book is the result of a legacy gift, a spiritual inheritance. I've been journaling for years but was never able to connect my yearning to that of my great grandmother and grandmother, who were scribes as well. My great grandmother Euzzie Norris was an international missionary and founding mother of the Church of our Lord Jesus Christ. Her legacy spanned the globe and was continued through my grandmother Althea Allen, who wrote powerfully, but in secret. It wasn't until 2013, when my father passed down the journals of my great grandmother and grandmother that I was able to connect my journey to their legacy. That connection was solidified when I read the passage above in my grandmother's journal.

While the idea for the book had come years earlier and the book had gone through several drafts by the time I read the passage, I realized that the title had been penned by my Grandmother decades earlier. A legacy delayed does not have to be denied. Although she was unable to share her thoughts during her lifetime, through this work, the words she penned live even beyond the grave.

May the circle be unbroken. Let the journey to the Beauty of Holiness begin!!!

Chapter 1
The Truth On Beauty

The portrayal of beauty varies across culture and time and is forever evolving and changing. In some cultures a long neck, either natural or enhanced, is considered beautiful. In others, we focus on the line of the nose or tininess of the feet. We can look to art for an understanding of cultural interpretations of beauty throughout history. Through the use of paintings, sculptures, and other artifacts, we are able to see the various ways beauty was appreciated and how sharply they contrast with our present ideals.

My sister and I love museums. It is always interesting to see what people of past generations looked like and how they dressed. While looking through art from previous years, we unconsciously judged their depictions of beauty in light of how it is portrayed in this day and time. My journey in understanding beauty led me to write the following poem:

I was a part of a painting whose canvas I did not choose, whose colors I would not use.

I was a part of a painting whose borders were too small, whose width was too thin and height was not tall.

I was a part of a painting whose strokes were too brief, scarring the intention of a rose with the reflection of a leaf.

I was a part of a painting whose brightness was dim, with texture too rough lacking smoothness of trim.

I was a part of a painting which was really a lie, showing others I said yes when I really asked why?

When observing beauty from a historical perspective, we see that the concept is not consistent and changes from one decade to the next. A culture can initially be fascinated by lips of a larger nature and then, some years later, be in favor of smaller ones. While technology or surgery can change some of the rules, we still lack total control over certain physical features. We cannot control the length of our arms or legs, or whether we have a short or long torso. Our DNA determines hair texture, eye color, skin pigment, and many other factors that make us who we are. It is from these factors, that are largely out of our control, that the characteristics of outward beauty are set. Yet it is all subjective, not only across time and culture, but individually as well. Our present culture tends to determine the beauty standard for us, and although we cannot control how our external features are judged, we alone have the power to determine the quality of our inner beauty.

Webster's dictionary defines beauty as the "quality or aggregate of qualities in a person or thing that gives pleasure to the senses or pleasurably exalts the mind or spirit." Notice this definition is holistic. It does not focus solely on external features, as we tend to do. It speaks to both the body and the soul. Synonyms for beauty include: attractiveness, cuteness, gorgeousness, looks, loveliness, and prettiness. These descriptions are a reflection of our current society, which ignores the internal components and only focuses on the external.

Today's beauty standards, influenced by print and media, are nearly impossible to attain. Women feel pressured to fit a beauty mold that is oftentimes created by airbrush software, plastic surgery, and other unnatural means. While some of these practices or means are minor, others are truly extreme. Too much emphasis on physical appearance can lead to unhealthy habits, such as anorexia, bulimia and other eating disorders. The billion-dollar beauty industry constantly focuses on the surface, our exterior, but there is actually more to real beauty than meets the eye.

The kind of beauty that is not based on our DNA is inner beauty, which comes through our heart and soul. This beauty is reflected through our mind, our will, emotions and attitude. It is one's character, which is the complexity of beliefs that shape a person's moral and ethical actions, reactions and behavior. This inner beauty is characterized by internal-focused words, such as sweet, kind, intelligence, and integrity. Since inner beauty is action-based, anyone can achieve it. Its definition is consistent over time and throughout cultures. It transcends the past, present and even the future.

For a true definition of beauty, an understanding of what our "best" selves look like, we should go to the Source. God has always known our hair type, eye color, height, character and personality. He created our being and released it into the world. He fashioned us knowing our outcome, and He sees us as beautiful.

I will praise thee; for I am fearfully and wonderfully made: marvelous are thy works.

-- Psalms 139:14

It is difficult for us to define and value what we do not fully understand. The true standard of beauty must come from God, the One who created us. When we go to Him, we can understand everything, even the small details of our construction.

3

I've heard people say of others, "She has such a sweet spirit." Isn't the word "sweet" generally used in relation to taste? However, they typically are not discussing how the person's spirit relates to their own sense of taste. Inner beauty is not a product of physicality, but we lack the tools to describe it any other way. So we discuss inner beauty with a different language than outer beauty. "Sweet" is no longer a physical sensation in this context. Sweet means this person does good or positive deeds. When we say, "She has a good heart," the physical heart is not the actual subject. The heart in this context is an observance of generous acts consistently demonstrated by an individual. The heart is a beauty mark that can be seen through actions, not physical features.

The Bible often omits extended descriptions of an individual's physical features. However, we are still able to determine their spiritual features. Much of what we learn of their "beauty" or lack thereof is from their actions, as we begin to discern the universal attributes of inner beauty. The way they respond to situations allows us to see their character, which is a reflection of the heart. Some personalities are sweet while others are malicious. Their true natures are not labeled up front but are revealed through different events. We will study several individuals in detail to provide a clear perspective of what is true beauty and what is not.

A person who is nice, kind and gentle is beautiful in spirit and a joy to be around. That beauty mark is a glow that starts inside and pushes beyond the internal until it radiates on the external. A person who is mean, bitter or angry is not pleasant to be around, and this also starts from the inside. Both individuals may have the same physical make up; however, it is their inner beauty that ultimately determines how those around them feel. Supermodel beauty cannot overshadow a negative spirit. Decide that when people look at you, the outside will radiate the greater beauty within you.

There was a point in my life when I had to be honest with myself. Throughout my life, people have often suggested that I should model. I pursued the modeling industry, which set me on a path to true self-discovery, finding out who I was and who God had fashioned me to be. It was hard to go into castings and hear someone say that my nose was too big or my skin was too dark. I actually like my nose because it is just like my dad's, and I have never considered my complexion in terms of darkness. The words and opinions of others caused me to question a lot about myself and how I defined beauty. I began looking at the complexion of others and compared it to mine. I also found myself comparing my facial features with others.

During this time I discovered the trap of allowing others to control my definition. Too many times we allow the opinions of others, even strangers, to define us. We are unable to see who we really are or want to be because we are constantly looking through the lenses of others. The blessing was that during this time I had also re-committed my life to Christ, and I had begun to study His Word. Through His Word I was able to dispel the thoughts that people had concerning me and focus on His thoughts. I was able to put away the lenses of their external definitions and put on the lenses of God's internal definitions.

I began to see myself through these new internal lenses. Although people considered me attractive, they were basing that on what they saw on the surface. I had internal traits that were ugly to God, which I had to correct. It was through this process that I learned the truly transcendent nature of inner beauty. My physical characteristics were not of my own choosing. They are the package through which God released me into the world. However, *I* have the choice and responsibility to change my internal characteristics. I could transform the ugliness of my heart and blossom in character and beauty through the Bible. In reading the Word and studying the scriptures, I was able to identify patterns I followed that brought ugly marks on my character and tarnished my inner beauty.

I realized when I talked about others and ran them down, my actions were reflecting my insecurities and jealousy. When others heard those words, they saw those marks on my character. These marks made me unattractive. More importantly, my actions were not pleasing to God. I was criticizing His creations, who He had fashioned in His own perfection. And in criticizing those creations, I was actually criticizing myself. Who was I to do such a thing? To tell God that His design was imperfect? I had to be honest and acknowledge that I struggled with low self-esteem. Although I was an athlete and a leader who many admired, I had many insecurities which caused me to have a low opinion of myself.

Unfortunately, all of these thoughts did not come from my own mind but also from negative words spoken by people I admired who were influential in my life. These negative perspectives inflicted deep wounds. These wounds became ugly marks, which I exposed when I spoke negatively and poorly of others. I heard it once said that when you point your finger, there are three fingers pointing back at you. I had to deal with those three fingers. When I started to grow and accept who I was as God's creation, I was able to begin to accept hard truths. Also, through reading and meditating on the Word, I was able to replace much of the negativity that I had accepted without question. I learned that I do not have to receive everything that is spoken about me. Some stuff you need to reject immediately. If not, it becomes a negative seed in your life which has the potential to grow. You cannot truly embrace others until you can truly embrace yourself.

When I became a makeup artist, my view of people was from God's lens and not my own. I began to see entirely different features as beautiful. The definition of beauty began to unfold like a flower. I saw physical traits that I could enhance, just like God saw characteristics in me that He wanted to enhance. As I beautified myself internally, I enjoyed helping others discover external features they could enhance and began to appreciate. I know what it's like to be criticized, and I know what it's like to be the one doing the criticizing. I made some internal adjustments and found joy in enhancing the beauty of others while encouraging them to highlight their internal beauty as well.

As women, many of us have come to our definition of beauty in a variety of ways. For some, our definition of beauty is based upon the opinions of others. Some of us have been blessed to have good influences that encouraged and positively affirmed us, assisting us in the development of good self-esteem. Some may not have had positive influences and are trying to find affirmation on their own. Unfortunately, even when the best of influences are in our corner, we may still have an internal struggle. We often accept others' definitions of beauty as fact. These definitions may have come from family, friends, coaches, teachers and even strangers. Some from people who claim that we would be more attractive "if…" If we were taller/shorter, smaller/thicker, lighter/darker, and the list goes on. Others have found their definition based on the type of people who were attracted to them or not attracted to them. A true definition does not change. It is established regardless of circumstance and situations. It is up to you to choose whose definition you will use.

I implore you to focus on God. External factors play a part in our development, but how much of a part they play is for us to decide. When we let external factors overpower us, add weight or burden to our lives, then those factors are controlling us. Webster's occasionally changes its definitions, but God's definition *never* changes. We must let His definition of beauty be our definition too, and keep the opinions of others in the appropriate place. It is a true balancing act for our beauty survival.

"Your beauty should not come from outward adornment, such as elaborate hairstyles and the wearing of gold jewelry or fine clothes. Rather, it should be that of your inner self, the unfading beauty of a gentle and quiet spirit, which is of great worth in God's sight."

--1 Peter 3:3-4 NIV

This is not saying you should totally disregard the external. It reveals what is greater in value—the inner self.

The parallel journey of people looking at me externally while God was looking at me internally helped me to see what beauty traits are most important. I remember an experience with a designer who wanted me to do some runway modeling for him, but said I had to lose weight first. So I worked out, but every time I went to see him, I still was not small enough. I finally realized that I would never fit his requirements, so I let the opportunity go. Meanwhile, when God showed me an internal flaw like gossiping, which does not match His beauty standards, I started

8

watching my words and conversation. God's standards were realistic, so my efforts in disciplining myself paid off. I was obedient and willing to allow my character to be developed, and now I am more beautiful to Him.

Write your personal definition of beauty below.

True beauty to me is having a heart and spirit that is aligned w/ Gods so that His light w/in you can radiate externally

Chapter 2
What Type of Skin Are You In?

*I*n my job as a makeup artist, the first thing clients want me to do is apply their makeup. Most never consider the condition of their skin first. They want the enhancements of makeup without properly caring for their skin. Makeup is a temporary enhancement; our skin is permanent. No matter how good the makeup artist is or how great they make you look, the makeup eventually has to be washed off.

In my journey as a Christian, many times I went to church but I didn't want to submit to the process it took to become like Christ. Like my clients, I wanted a quick fix. I enjoyed listening to the sermons and the music, but didn't always apply what I had heard. As I began to study the Word of God, I realized that there was no quick fix. A lifestyle change was required.

Just as we have to take care of our natural skin, we have to take care of our hearts, which for the purpose of this book, is also known as your spiritual skin. It consists of the mind, will, emotions and attitude. These areas require daily attention just like our external skin requires daily maintenance. But, in order to determine a cleansing regimen, the skin type must first be determined.

There are five different skin types: oily, dry, combination, sensitive and normal. Skin type is determined by how much—or how little—oil the skin produces, and can also be determined by looking at the skin's features. Genes, diet, stress level, medication and even our skincare regimen, all determine how much oil our skin produces. [1]

As you read the following descriptions ask yourself: *What type of skin am I in?*

Oily Skin

It has been said that some ethnicities are more prone to oily skin than others, but that is a myth. Oily skin affects all ethnicities, ages and sexes. Oily skin requires the maximum care as it is prone to acne, pimples and breakouts. Oily skin enlarges the pores and causes blemishes. The oil can be found in what is called the T-zone (across the forehead and down the nose).[2] Oily skin is caused by overactive sebaceous glands that produce a substance called sebum, a natural healthy skin lubricant. When the skin produces excessive sebum, it becomes heavy and thick in texture. Oily skin can be sallow and rough in texture and tends to have large, clearly visible pores everywhere—except around the eyes and neck.[3]

Spiritually, we all start off with oily skin when we are born. Although God knows who we are, discovering and knowing who He is to us, takes time. Until that connection takes place, many of the things we do don't line up with the Word of God. From birth we are bombarded with making choices between good and evil, what pleases God versus what displeases God. When we live a life that does not please God, it produces oily skin. The enemy tempts us through these oils and when we take the bait, he traps us in sins of perversion, lust, lying, hate, jealousy, pride and the list goes on and on, giving us spiritual blackheads and blemishes. These blemishes lead to shame, embarrassment and guilt. Although we start with oily skin, we do have an opportunity to change. Change starts with making the decision to choose Christ as your personal Lord and Savior. Some have been given the opportunity but have not made a decision; others have made the decision but are not fully walking in what they know is right. We are born oily but we don't have to remain oily.

Naturally, it's easy to determine if you have oily skin. Simply wipe your face with a tissue before washing your face in the morning. If there are traces of oil on the tissue, then you have oily skin. Spiritually, you know if you have oily skin by the buildup of that which displeases God in your conversations, thoughts and actions.

Dry Skin

Dry skin has a thin texture, looks visibly dry, and requires much care. Dry skin feels tight, especially after cleansing. People with dry skin tend to have fine wrinkles, flaking, and red patches. In some ethnicities, dry skin may appear ashy or dull from dead skin buildup. Dry skin also peels. It can be itchy and irritated by fabrics and weather changes.[4] Different elements like the sun can cause the skin to peel and sometimes crack. Dry skin hardens very easily. Many with dry skin feel the dryness more acutely than may be indicated by the appearance of it. For some, dry skin can be noticeable and embarrassing.

Spiritually speaking, a person with dry skin can feel as if life has been sucked out of them. Their emotional walls are thin, leaving them with feelings of hopelessness, desperation and depression. Nothing seems stable; it appears as if everything they put their hands to falls apart. The dryness causes dullness and emotional buildup. These buildups can develop from disappointment, loss, misfortune and failure, which cause spiritual fine wrinkles. Spiritually dry skin causes one to hold onto the past. Even when new opportunities are provided for them, they remain spiritually stagnant. The emotional entanglement seem impossible to break free from. It seems easier to stay in a lifeless situation than step into something better that is unfamiliar. Strong attachments to people, places and things cause a fear of new beginnings. This is equivalent to the natural tightness felt with dry skin; it does not allow for flexibility. This skin type is easily aggravated, annoyed, and typically responds in anger.

Combination Skin

Combination skin is considered the most common skin type. This skin type has average sized pores, a smooth and even texture, good circulation, healthy color, and may tend toward dryness on the cheeks while being oily in the T-zone. Combination skin could be considered the toughest skin type to conquer because you could be dealing with two opposite ends of the skincare spectrum. The majority of people with combination skin have a T-zone that is oily and cheeks that are dry. Many people have to deal with occasional breakouts and larger than normal pores, particularly on the nose.[5]

Spiritually, combination skin can be observed as being in more than one category. You have been making decisions in the right direction however there are inconsistencies in your spiritual skin. Spiritually the pores are not as big in some areas because of your decision to follow Christ. Your spiritual skin has been refined in some areas. Yet other areas may still be an issue, which causes spiritual dry patches. You are still being changed, and through this process you may still have an oily spiritual T-zone, caused by "oily" thoughts (negative feelings, perceptions and ideas). This T-zone area is one of the most important challenges because it directs your course in life—what you think and act on.

Sensitive Skin

This skin type is sensitive to dirt, dust, the sun and other allergens. It itches, and has redness and patches. It may sometimes react immediately when affected by agitation or soreness in an area. Sensitive skin tends to be thin and delicate with fine pores. It flushes easily, is prone to broken capillaries, frequently allergic, and can be rashy.[6] This skin type requires much care and must be treated gently and delicately. Sensitive skin is not receptive to many new treatments, for fear of how the skin will respond. It takes a great deal to stabilize this particular skin type.

Spiritually, sensitive skin can belong to someone suffering with complex and delicate issues. It sometimes causes one to react irrationally out of fear that a sensitive area will be touched. Different parts of their emotions are fragmented and even damaged. They have been emotionally injured and need healing. They've experienced many broken relationships and frequently overreact to situations. Typically a person with this spiritual skin type has deep emotional wounds and is not open to new relationships or experiences.

Normal Skin

Normal skin is balanced, smooth and easy to care for.[7] This skin type does well in all weather and has very few breakouts or reactions. Both naturally and spiritually, normal skin is ideal.

Spiritually, normal skin is viewed as someone who has an established relationship with God. They reflect the ways of God and are obedient to the Word of God. They have been challenged but they are overcomers. They live a balanced life. A person with normal skin is

14

seasoned not by age, but by spiritual maturity. We all age, but we don't all mature. They are faithful, committed, and strive for perfection in God.

Blessed is the one who does not walk in step with the wicked or stand in the way that sinners take or sit in the company of mockers, ²but whose delight is in the law of the Lord, and who meditates on his law day and night³ That person is like a tree planted by streams of water, which yields its fruit in season and whose leaf does not wither whatever they do prospers.

-- Psalm 1:1-3

As you can see from the scripture above, this is a person who makes wise decisions regarding who they connect with and where they go. They take responsibility for their actions. In order for trees to yield fruit, the roots must go deep, which indicates maturity gained through the experience of seasons (different points in time).

Life experiences can leave us damaged and prevent us from operating properly. It's like a car that has been in an accident. If the door was hit, it may still open, but it may not function the way it was made to. The owner must take the car to the body shop to correct the problem. Many of us need to go to the Spiritual body shop and get the maintenance and care needed so we can run and function like God intended. Are you in need of maintenance?

Review the definitions of the five basic skin types below. After an honest heart evaluation, answer the question: What type of skin type do I have, both naturally and spiritually? The questions below are designed to help you determine which category you belong to. Accept what you discover. Do not condemn or beat yourself up. Truth is the first step on the journey to freedom and healing.

Natural Skin Type	Spiritual Skin Type
Oily - tends to be shiny with enlarged pores and is prone to blackheads and blemishes. You may experience some tightness.	**Oily** - sin is still very active in one's life.
Dry - skin feels tight, especially after cleansing. Skin is prone to fine wrinkles, flaking and red patches. In women of color, skin may appear ashy or dull from dead skin buildup.	**Dry** - hopelessness, depression, life seems to always be falling apart, unstable.
Combination - has medium pores, a smooth and even texture, good circulation, healthy color, prone to dryness on the cheeks while oily in the T-zone.	**Combination** - mixture of skin types. Relationship with Christ is strong in some areas, yet noticeably weak in others.
Sensitive - tends to be thin, delicate with fine pores. It flushes easily, is prone to broken capillaries; is frequently allergic and prone to rashes.	**Sensitive** - suffers from complex and delicate issues.
Normal - balanced, smooth and easy to care for.	**Normal** - strong relationship with Christ through obedience to the Word of God.

1. Does your skin have rough or smooth areas?

2. Are your words hurtful or do your words promote healing?

3. Is your skin tone even or discolored?

4. Is your spiritual walk smooth or bumpy?

5. How sensitive is your face to the elements?

6. Are you easily offended or hurt?

7. What different types of acne do you have, or have had in the past?

8. What sins are you most vulnerable to? Anger, impatience, self-pity, arrogance or _____?

9. Where does acne affect you the most on your face?

10. What areas does sin affect you the most: financially, emotionally, physically or other?

11. Do you experience a lot of burning, chafing and redness in your skin?

12. How do you avoid sin in your life?

13. Does your beauty routine require low or high maintenance to keep your looking skin healthy?

14. How is your spiritual discipline?

15. Do you touch, pick or mark your face?

16. Do you continually entertain sin?

17. How much time do you spend in the elements (ie: the sun)?

18. How much time do you spend in the Bible?

19. What are your skin concerns?

20. Are you willing to grow spiritually?

Odd numbers = natural application

Even numbers = spiritual application

Chapter 3
Skin Care 101

Now that we have identified our skin type, we can select a cleansing system to meet our skin care needs. Over the years I have bought so many skin care products that I would be rich if I had purchased stock in certain companies instead. Much of what I bought was due to effective advertising, recommendations and word of mouth.

All skin types need a cleansing regimen. The elements can vary based on the skin type, but the basics remain the same. A basic natural skin cleansing regimen—regardless of skin type—consists of: cleanser, toner, moisturizer and exfoliation. How much and how often to use each product is determined by the skin type. In comparison, a spiritual cleansing regimen consists of: studying the Word, prayer and repentance, praise and worship, and fasting.

Daily face washing is crucial regardless of age or skin type. You should thoroughly wash your face at least twice a day: once in the morning and once in the evening. This helps to keep your skin healthy and balanced.

Likewise, you should cleanse your spirit in the morning and in the evening to keep your spirit pure. Whether you have been saved for thirty years or for thirty minutes, whether your walk is solid or shaky, it is crucial that you cleanse your spiritual skin every day. You must have a daily spiritual cleansing regimen because the impurities of this world must be constantly and consistently removed.

Practical Application

Apply the cleanser.[8] Cleansers remove any impurities, makeup residue and oils which, if not removed, can lead to serious skin problems such as clogged pores, blackheads, whiteheads, pimples and discoloration. Oil secretion is a sign of the body cleansing itself. Many cleansers specialize and specify what skin type they work best on. Most cleansers have key ingredients to target skin issues associated with a particular skin type.

A good facial cleanser is beneficial regardless of the skin type. Cleansers help remove dirt and debris and eliminate surface bacteria. It reduces oil secretions and provides a soothing sensation to the skin while excess toxins are removed, resulting in a fresh skin texture. When using a cleanser, do not wash off the cleanser immediately after applying it. Let it penetrate your skin for a few minutes, then remove it.

Spiritually, the Word of God cleanses our spirit. The Word exposes sin and character flaws, while revealing ways to mature, and corrections we need to make. The Word can replace negative mindsets, evil thoughts and contrary ways with Truth, which is pure, holy and lovely. Don't just read the Word, meditate on it. Meditating on the Word will help you have pure thoughts.

Finally, brethren, whatsoever things are true, whatsoever things are honest, whatsoever things are just, whatsoever things are pure, whatsoever things are lovely, whatsoever things are of good report; if there be any virtue, and if there be any praise, think on these things.

--Philippians 4:8

19

Meditating on the Word is also the pathway to receive instructions from God. Meditation in the midst of trying situations allows God to speak a scripture or remind us of a passage or sermon that will bring clarity and give direction for a positive outcome.

A boss from a previous job was not very nice and extremely negative, which made for a hostile work environment. In order to stay balanced, I had to read my Bible before work and during lunchtime to make sure I kept the right attitude. One day my boss called me into her office where she and another manager proceeded to berate me. I was heated to say the least, but because I had meditated on the Word earlier, I kept silent and demonstrated self-control. I'm not saying it was easy, but by mediating on the Word, I was able to successfully buffer the negativity directed toward me. Moral of the story: study the Word and use it as a lifestyle instruction manual.

So that thou incline thine ear unto wisdom, and apply thine heart to understanding.

-- Proverbs 2:2

In studying the Bible, we discover many people had flaws just like we do. We can learn from their mistakes and use the instructions provided to them to benefit our own lives. Every situation we need help with or instruction for is covered in the Bible, but we must actively pursue learning what God has to say through the written Word.

Having therefore these promises, dearly beloved, let us cleanse ourselves from all filthiness of the flesh and the spirit, perfecting holiness in the fear of God.

-- 2 Corinthians 7:1

The Word of God is saturated with God's promises toward us. His Word is filled with all the wonderful thoughts and plans He has for us. All that's required of us is to first believe His Word and then obey it wholeheartedly. We must desire spiritual cleanliness and make every effort to maintain it.

Tone Your Skin

Toners remove traces of makeup, dirt and oil that the cleanser may have missed. Toners also reduce pore size, eliminate oil and refine the skin. Toners balance the ph level of the skin.

Spiritually toners are a two part process which includes prayer and repentance. In allowing us to clarify and ask for assistance in areas where our reading hasn't fully settled, prayer brings strength, just like toners tighten our pores. Prayer is our communication line to God. It allows us to present our petitions and to cry out to Him. Prayer is simply talking to God and expressing our thoughts, feelings and emotions. Prayer is the channel through which deliverance and healing flows.

As E.M. Bounds explains:

Prayer changes the one praying because in prayer, you are in the presence of God as you lay before Him your complete self in confession and dependence. There is nothing to hide when in quiet supplication we are reaching into the deepest part of ourselves and admitting our needs and failures.[9]

Prayer produces a barrier around you and in you. It refines your spirit man and helps you to become more like Christ. It is the outward and upward flow of the inward life towards its original fountain.[10] As we connect to God, who is the original fountain, prayer causes a pure stream of the spirit of God to freely flow. Prayer brings a balance to the inward life, which consist of our mind, will, and emotions. When we submit these to God in prayer, we can be cleansed and purified. As every day demands its bread, so every day demands its prayer.[11]

The Bible is filled with examples of the power of prayer. Throughout the sixty-six books, people from every economic and social status cried out to God: kings, priests, warriors, prophets, widows and servants, just to name a few. We may not always know what to say, but we can use their examples as a model for our personal prayers. Prayer should be a two-way conversation. Although we may have a lot to say, make sure to allot time to listen as well.

I was blessed to have grown up in a Christian home. On Tuesday nights after a short sermon, we would all go into the prayer room. After getting a kneeling blanket, we would choose our bench and get on our knees to pray. In listening to my father pray, I patterned my prayers with some of his words and then began to share with God what was on my heart.

Hear my prayer, O God; give ear to the words of my mouth.

--Psalm 54:2

The above scripture is a great way to open a prayer. It is simplistic, yet intense. The book of Psalms is loaded with various situational prayers, well suited for the varying situations of our own lives. Depending on our present circumstances, our prayers will differ in length, approach and intensity. There is no wrong way to execute a prayer. We just need to open our mouth and speak.

Evening, and morning, and at noon, will I pray, and cry aloud: and he shall hear my voice.

--Psalm 55:17

Prayer is something we can do at any time and all the time. The blessing is, God never slumbers or sleeps. He is available 24/7 and no appointment is necessary. Simply open your mouth and speak.

But verily God hath heard me; he hath attended to the voice of my prayer.

--Psalm 66:19

Oftentimes we feel like we are talking and God is not listening. This scripture assures us that He does hear and He does respond to the prayers we set before him. However, since we are unable to determine when the answer to our prayer will come, we just have to trust and believe that it will be answered.

Prayer leads to repentance. Repentance, like toner, cleanses our souls of the traces of sin left behind after cleansing and builds the weak areas in our lives through faith. Repentance should also be a part of our daily cleansing regimen. True repentance releases Satan's control over our lives and unclogs our spiritual pores by eliminating the oils of sin. Repentance means to make an about face, to turn away. When we truly repent we turn away from sin and move toward the things of God. Many of us repent with our mouths, but do not follow through with corresponding actions. Repentance requires our mouth, heart and soul to be in agreement. When we truly repent we will shun the slightest appearance of evil.

Repentance is not a dramatic performance or traumatic experience. Sincere repentance is simply asking for forgiveness with the intent to never repeat the action again. In some ways repentance is as easy as saying, "I'm sorry." For example, if you bump into someone, apologize. If your actions are offensive, take responsibility for your actions and ask for forgiveness.

As toner prepares the skin for the moisturizer, prayer and repentance prepares us for praise and worship.

Moisturize

Moisturizers hydrate the skin and stop impurities from penetrating the skin. Moisturizers also help to maintain suppleness and moisture. Basic law of beauty: everyone, no matter the skin type, should moisturize. Even if your skin is oily, it will benefit from a moisturizer.

Spiritually, praise and worship seals in the Word we have read, the prayers we have prayed, and helps us to maintain our walk and communion with the Father. It is the finishing touch. Praise and worship liberates us to express our love for Him freely, and He expresses His love back to us. Webster's dictionary defines praise as "the ability to express adoration of, approval and commendation." When we offer praise to God, we communicate our approval and thankfulness for Him. Praise has different forms: affection, affirmation, and gratitude amongst others.

Praise leads us into worship where we show our love for God through obedience and by living the life He has revealed through the

Bible. Worship is a form of humility, reverence and honor. When we worship we surrender our will to His leading and guidance. We honor God for who He is through worship. Our lifestyle should be one of worship, honoring and obeying God in every aspect.

I will bless the LORD at all times: his praise shall continually be in my mouth.

-- Psalm 34:1

In this verse the writer takes the position that he will live a life of blessing the Lord, and he will do it at all times. This is definitely an example we should follow. With praise continually in our mouth, we release less negativity. Praise exemplifies a heart of thanksgiving and gratitude.

O come, let us worship and bow down: let us kneel before the LORD our maker.

-- Psalm 95:6

Worship is the time when we acknowledge God's power and authority. It's when we bestow honor and reverence from a place of humility. To bow represents a humbled position. Although many people physically bow when worshipping, it's essential to "bow" spiritually. The condition of our heart is more important than physical alignment.

Exfoliate

Don't forget to exfoliate your skin once or twice a week to remove dead skin cells. Exfoliation encourages a newer, smoother skin surface by helping to unclog pores, which prevents further breakouts and diminishes blemishes and pigmentation spots. Exfoliation is the step most people skip in their weekly skincare routine. If you properly exfoliate your skin, you will notice an immediate difference. There are different types of exfoliations; some are more intense than others. These include scrubs, peels and microdermabrasion.

Spiritually, fasting is our exfoliation. Fasting brings our flesh under subjection to the will of God and strengthens our spirit man as we continually shed ourselves of the old man. Fasting unclogs hidden sins, strengthens our discernment, and erases the stain of ungodliness. The discoloration of actions that were not pleasing to God are removed.

Is not this the fast that I have chosen? To loose the bands of wickedness, to undo the heavy burdens, and to let the oppressed go free, and that ye break every yoke?

-- Isaiah 58:6

This illustrates the results of fasting. Areas in our lives which have bound us are loosed. Heavy burdens are released. Those who are oppressed are set free. Yokes, things which enslave us, are broken.

But thou, when thou fastest, anoint thine head, and wash thy face, That thou appear not unto men to fast, but unto thy Father which is in secret: and thy Father, which seeth in secret, shall reward thee openly.

-- Matthew 6:17,18

Fasting is intimate time with God. It is private and very personal, which is why Jesus provided the above guidelines. In biblical times,

26

some people made themselves look dreary so everyone would know they were fasting. They sought sympathy. Here, Jesus clearly states we should practice good hygiene and conduct ourselves in the same manner as if we were not fasting at all. In obeying these commands, He lets us know there is a reward that comes through fasting.

Some strongholds will only be removed from our life through fasting. God is a master surgeon, and He knows how to eradicate sin, weights and burdens from our lives. When we fast, He reveals the hidden things in our heart that are not like Him. Fasting is similar to using a fog bomb in your house to kill bugs. On the surface you may see a few, but most of them can stay hidden in the walls. Sometimes we see some sins actively operating in our lives while other sins are hidden in our hearts. Fasting unlocks sins of the heart, which we cannot easily see.

Spiritually, there are different types of fasting. A traditional fast involves eating no food, only drinking water or juice. A partial fast is abstaining from specific foods for a predetermined period of time. The time and duration of a fast can vary from once a week to forty days. Before starting a fast, it is imperative to seek God's direction for the type of fast and also the length of the fast. Also use wisdom. If you take medication or have health issues, get medical clearance based on your condition—especially for an extended fast.

Many times when we walk down the beauty aisle in a store, we are not sure what to look for. The information above has provided a standard set of beauty products we all need regardless of skin type. This will help in determining what you need to add or subtract from your cabinet. Again, regardless of skin type, we need to cleanse, tone, moisturize and exfoliate. You should also stock up your spiritual cabinet.

Every believer needs to incorporate a regimen of the Word of God, prayer and repentance, praise and worship, and fasting.

Now that you are able to see what is needed naturally and spiritually, and the order in which these tools should be used, you can start your cleansing regimen anew. You *will* begin to see favorable results when you regularly apply these disciplines. A new you is awaiting. Let the expedition begin!

Chapter 4
What's on the Weather Channel?

As a Florida native I know all about extreme heat, humidity and hurricanes. I was taught all about summer: however, I didn't fully understand the concept of the four seasons. When I moved to Illinois, I was inducted into a life of four seasons. I moved in the summer and experienced a very short fall and a very long winter. One of the first things I realized was that I needed a full wardrobe. You can't wear the same clothes year round when you have four seasons.

My skin also responded differently. The environment drastically affected me during the seasonal changes, and I had to make the necessary adjustments. When winter time came, I had to change the products I used due to the severe cold. In Illinois we are not just subject to the cold, but the severe winds, which can sometimes exceed 30 miles per hour. In fact, the wind is so strong they named it "The Hawk." With such weather extremities, I went from using a lotion-based moisturizer to a thick cream to ensure my skin was fully moisturized. In the spring, I kept the cream moisturizer because the winds in Chicago are still harsh despite the warmer temperature. I didn't have to make these types of drastic adjustment while I was in Florida.

I learned that depending on the season, more or less skin care would be needed. It takes much effort to care for our skin, both naturally and spiritually. The first thing we must do is determine what season we are in—winter, spring, summer or fall.

In winter the weather is harsh. Temperatures can be frigid and elements like sleet and snow are problematic. Winter is a time when

29

things seem to be stuck, frozen, and lack momentum. Spiritually, you may be experiencing a time of loss; a shedding from the old and familiar. The elements can also be more extreme and dangerous. Times and seasons are not to be ignored. In Ecclesiastes 3 we learn there is a time for everything.

There is a time for everything, and a season for every activity under the heavens:

> *a time to be born and a time to die, a time to plant and a time to uproot,*
> *a time to kill and a time to heal, a time to tear down and a time to build,*
> *a time to weep and a time to laugh, a time to mourn and a time to dance,*
> *a time to scatter stones and a time to gather them, a time to embrace and a time to refrain from embracing,*
> *a time to search and a time to give up, a time to keep and a time to throw away,*
> *a time to tear and a time to mend, a time to be silent and a time to speak,*
> *a time to love and a time to hate, a time for war and a time for peace.*

--Ecclesiastes 3:1-9

Let us now discover how to care for both our natural and spiritual skin based on the season we are in.

Seasonal Skin Care

Natural Winter

During winter all skin types require more moisture. A good moisturizer provides a shield and a barrier against harsh elements. To combat the extreme temperatures, some people change from a lotion to a cream, which has a stronger concentration. You can also use a creamier cleanser, which provides additional moisture and ensures that your skin is well balanced.

Spiritual Winter[12]

Our spiritual winter is a time of gaining clarity. There may not be as much movement during this season. You can really take inventory of where you are, where you should be and what to do to get there. Spiritual winter is the most uncomfortable time for many Christians. We might feel that God has deserted us during this season, but this is the time to curl up in God's lap for warmth and intimacy. There He will give you direction for planting new crops to harvest in the next season— spring. It is also the time to be strengthened by what has been stored up from previous harvests.

Winter is the time for evaluation, planning and preparation. It is the time to shovel snow and ice from the driveway of your mind. It is the time to learn to navigate the icy roads as you go about your business. Shoveling is not a passive action. It takes a lot of hard work and effort. When shoveling snow from your mind, you are discarding thoughts and opinions of others, which have no value. You must be committed to keeping clarity. The icy road represents slippery situations, which need to be handled properly; if not, they can cause damage. It is the time wh praise should be an automatic habit. It will keep your heart warm before a Holy God.

During spiritual winter, it is normal to feel like God is not hearing our prayers or speaking to us. We may feel like we are having a "wilderness" experience. However, it is a time of spiritual rest. It's the perfect time to reflect on God and His faithfulness to you, and to maintain an attitude of reverence before Him. Winter is also the time to PLAN for the upcoming seasons.

Natural Spring

In spring your skin care needs change because of the wide range of warm and cool days. You literally have to make adjustments to your cleansing regimen based on the daily weather forecast.

Spiritual Spring[13]

Spring is a time of activity, a time of work and effort to carry out the instructions received in winter. It is also a renewal of dreams and hope, a time of awakening. It is a time of great spiritual and physical energy. One should spend time plowing new and sometimes hard ground, and take time to fertilize the soil with prayer. Having spent time with God, you will have the spiritual and physical energy to break up the fallow ground or problematic areas in your personal life.

Spring is the time to come out of the stillness of winter. You will see the first signs of vigor and life returning to the earth. Spring reminds us of the eternal cycle of death and rebirth and renewed life. Spring is the re-emergence of life. It exemplifies the balance between growth and decay, youth and maturity, innocence and experience.

During springtime, look for the leading of the Holy Spirit in new activities, ventures and opportunities. These can be activities like new ways of doing your daily devotionals or opportunities to develop new relationships.

Natural Summer

Summer is a season of exfoliation. Exfoliation should take place on a regular basis regardless of the season, but especially during the summer to remove excess build-up. For those with oily skin, make sure you use toner to take care of the excess oils.

Spiritual Summer[14]

Summer is a time of watering (praying) the freshly planted crop. It is a time in which the crop is in potential danger from the heat of summer, thus the need for much watering. It is also the time when we begin to see the first evidence of our planting. This is a time of fasting for spiritual exfoliation. Summer is a time of both growth and of stillness; of hard work in the fields and of relaxing in the cool of the day.

Summer is the time to pause and reflect. It is the time to play, relax and enjoy some leisure time after you have planted your seeds. It is a time to plow up and cultivate the soil. In summer the flowers are in full bloom. The fruit is ripe and ready to be picked. It is during this spiritual season that we develop the fruit of the Spirit. We read in Galatians 5:22 "But the fruit of the Spirit is love, joy, peace, patience, kindness, goodness, faithfulness, gentleness and self–control." Are any of these qualities exhibited in your life?

Natural Fall

In the fall, your skin is generally balanced because the elements are not too harsh at this time. Keeping the normal routine will help maintain your skin.

Spiritual Fall[15]

Fall is the time of harvest; a time when the physical evidence of our hard work during previous seasons is revealed. It is a time of thanksgiving and a time of refreshing. Fall is a time for storing up for the winter that is sure to come. Fall is a time of utilizing good stewardship and proper disbursement of what has been harvested.[16]

Provided you have been diligent during the previous seasons, fall is the time of harvest. Without the ability to accurately discern the season you are in, you will miss many opportunities. When you are aware of the season you are in, you will be able to step into new spiritual truths and obtain a greater ability to flow in the power of God. Fall, with its colorful trees, is the transitional season that mirrors both the abundance and the limitation of our everyday lives. Fall helps us see the passage of time; where we have come from and where we need to go. This is the season filled with anticipation. If we have been obedient in the prior seasons, we will reap a harvest in due season. Fall is a time of fruition and reaping, thanksgiving and celebrating the abundance and goodness of nature. It is a season of encouragement as we witness the changes in God's earth.

Please note that seasons vary in time frame, both in the natural and spiritual. When watching the weather channel, you can see some states look like they are in summer during the month of December while others are experiencing an extreme winter. The month may be the same but the experience is totally different. This is why location is also important. You can be on a mountain or in a valley, on a hill or leveled land. Your location would also dictate making adjustments to your skincare regimen. If you are high in the mountains, the air can be dry, which would require more moisture. If you are on a hill, the sun could be beaming, which would require more toning of the skin. Spiritually, when you are on the mountain, you may need more worship. If you are on a hill, you may need more prayer.

The elements can also change how you handle yourself spiritually. Sunshine could represent that your prayers are being answered. On the other hand, if it's raining, you may need to pray more. A thunderstorm could mean you need to fast, because you are being tested. A spiritual hurricane could signify you are in a battle and need to intensify the essentials of prayer, praise and worship, fasting and reading the Word.

Caring for your spiritual skin requires that you to pay attention to both the natural and spiritual weather channel. The more you are aware, the easier it is to prepare and properly care for your skin.

Chapter 5
Skin Care Myths, Truths & Mistakes

There are many myths floating around concerning natural skincare. So many, that I can't list them all in one chapter. Many myths exist for spiritual skincare as well. Interestingly, some natural myths are actually spiritual truths. We will examine and dispel some of the more common misguided beliefs and establish the truth.

Myth vs Truth

1.   Chocolate, Pizza, French Fries and Acne[17]

Acne is not just a problem for teens, but teens tend to consume more of the foods thought by many to cause acne, such as chocolate and fried foods. I am happy to let you know that acne is not caused by what we eat. Acne is caused by overactive sebaceous glands, which clog pores and produce acne. While you don't want to eat an abundance of fried or greasy foods, feel free to have that piece of pizza or occasional candy bar with the peace of mind that eating these foods will **not** cause acne.

Spiritually, however, the reverse is true. When we eat spiritual junk food, we put our souls at risk. Spiritual junk food includes: television shows that promote lust and greed, reading sexually explicit or violently graphic novels, and speaking evil of others, to name a few. Although natural junk food will not cause acne, spiritual junk food plants seeds of sin in our hearts and minds. When sin is acted upon and the seed sprouts, it causes a spiritual breakout. Make an effort to keep your spiritual skin clear and free of breakouts.

2.   You Don't Wash Your Face Enough

For good skin care, we should wash our face twice a day: once in the morning and once at night. People often assume that people with acne don't wash their face enough. This is incorrect thinking. Acne comes from far below the skin's surface. If you are washing your face in the morning and before bed, you're doing all the right steps. If midday oil is a problem, use oil-blotting sheets.

Spiritually, someone prone to acne breakouts should incorporate an aggressive regimen. Sin begins with a thought that is contrary to God's Word. The thought can come from an external party; however, many times it comes from within, through our thoughts, feelings and emotions. The thought then becomes an action that can evolve into a repetitive action, until it becomes a habit then, ultimately, part of one's character. When we continually practice sin, we become comfortable with that sin and it sprouts through our spiritual skin like acne.

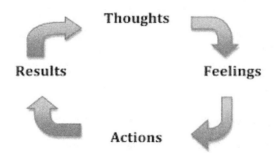

Thoughts

Results

Feelings

Actions

A person with a severe case of spiritual acne requires deliverance to set them free from spiritual bondage. The enemy has lied to all of us in one way or another. These lies can come through thoughts of our own or from outside sources. When we believe the lies, it puts us in spiritual bondage. These bonds are not easily broken free from because they are repeatedly wrapped around us, just like our sins that have become a repetitive cycle. Deliverance is the process through which those thoughts, those cycles, are broken and we are set free by God.

Many times the reason we keep having "spiritual break outs" is because the root issue is never dealt with. Deliverance will clear out the spiritual bacterium that causes the breakouts. When going through the deliverance process, it is often a good time to fast to ensure that our flesh, or base desires, is not in control. Regular spiritual exfoliation is necessary for preventative care of spiritual acne.

3.   Nothing Will Get Rid of Acne

If you're dealing with acne and you truly believe nothing will get rid of it, I've got good news for you: your acne is treatable if you find the right products and medicines. I highly recommend a visit to a dermatologist for a skin evaluation. If it is a severe case, why waste money on over the counter products that may not work for you? Let the experts decide what's best for your skin. You may need a new skincare regimen, antibiotics or even stronger prescriptions to remove your acne, but you will never know if you don't go.

Jesus is our physician. And when we repent, He forgives us and no longer remembers our sins.

If we confess our sins, he is faithful and just to forgive us our sins and to cleanse us from all unrighteousness.

-- 1 John 1:19

Jesus' prescription causes all unrighteousness, which is wrongfulness in character or life, to be forgiven when we sincerely repent (change our thinking and behavior). Spiritual acne can result from unforgiveness and bitterness. Many times we have such deep hurts that it's hard for us to forgive. Unforgiveness affects us spiritually and can even affect our physical bodies. In most cases we must forgive ourselves before we can forgive others. The joy is in knowing that we can be freed from unforgiveness and, as we get free, we can release others. Then the blotches of unforgiveness on our spiritual skin will begin to fade away.

Skin Care Mistakes

1.   Using Water Alone to Hydrate Your Skin[18]

Water is essential for the face, but other elements are needed to hydrate the skin as well. Moisturizers provide ingredients and vitamins, which absorb into the skin to bring hydration and some essential elements to nourish the skin. These elements provide a lasting effect on the skin.

There are elements that are also essential for our spiritual skin to be nourished. A church service provides an atmosphere of praise and worship, and hearing the Word of God preached. Praise and Worship are the moisturizers that hydrate our spiritual skin. These elements are part of the spiritual skin care regimen, but church shouldn't be the only time they are used. Some people think just because they attend church, they are fine. This is not the case. We should not make praise and worship service the only time we work on building an intimate relationship with God.

Unfortunately, this is exactly what many people do. They go to church on Sunday, and that is the only time they worship or acknowledge God. Building a solid relationship requires both time and commitment. We must spend time reading His Word. This is how we learn His ways, character and will. Most of us would not like it if someone we loved only communicated with us sporadically. It is the same with God. We have access to speak with Him or praise Him at any time. He is so in love with us that He waits patiently on our call, and when we call He is there to answer.

Spending time with God can be as simple as listening to worship music while getting ready for work and praying to Him while driving. These are just two examples of how to develop a closer relationship with God.

Have you ever really wanted to get to know someone? Something about them intrigued you. When the connection is made, you have such an expectation because you have been waiting for this moment. Well, God already knows us, and He desires for us to know Him. He is just waiting for that moment we decide to spend time with Him so He can show us who He really is.

2.   Using Someone Else's Skin Care Products

Everyone needs a cleansing regimen, but you have to use what is best for your particular skin type. Many people share the same skin type; however, products affect people differently, and you have to find the product that works right for you.

Spiritually, your relationship with God is personal and should not be compared with anyone else's. Although we are all on a journey, we must know individually what we need for our trip. You may be in a season where you need more worship, while a friend who has the same spiritual skin type may need more of the Word, due to the season that they are in. You need to know where you are in God. What God may be working on in another person may not be an issue for you. Your regimen has to be personal and customized.

3.   Picking Your Blemishes

Picking at your acne exacerbates the problem. It disturbs the wall of the skin and also causes the bacteria from the acne to spread. Excessive picking can cause an infection. Instead, use products that reduce the swelling and allow the skin to heal in its own time.

It is best to keep your hands off of spiritual acne. To pick a spiritual blemish is to continually entertain sin. We are to flee from sin, not play with it. Temptations can come, but we do not have to act on them; we can walk away. For example, if a married man shows interest in you, run away! Run as fast as you can! That is a situation you don't play with. I know women who have not walked away and, subsequently, have entered into relationships with married men. They are picking at a huge blemish. They thought they were strong enough to handle a man being dedicated to someone else, but it affected their self-esteem and sent them on an emotional rollercoaster. Playing with this blemish eventually causes a serious spiritual infection.

We all know about relationships where the couple makes up and breaks up constantly for years. The relationship may be official for three months then they're separated for two months, then back together for seven months, then separated five months, and on and on. Obviously, this is not healthy; it is the spiritual equivalent of picking a blemish. When you close the door on a hurtful situation or negative issue, your spiritual skin can now enter the healing process. If you re-open that door, it's like picking the skin, welcoming back that issue, and making it harder to close it off again. The more you pick at the skin, the longer it will take to heal.

Skin Journeys

I went through a time when I allowed makeup to define my beauty. I would not leave the house without makeup on. If I didn't do a full face, I at least had to do my eyebrows. One of the main reasons I wore makeup was because my combination skin left discolorations from the blackheads and blemishes. To me, they were so apparent I wanted to keep them hidden. I didn't feel comfortable until every mark was covered. Eventually, I was put on a path of discovery and challenged to wear no makeup at all. When I was stripped of wearing makeup, it forced me to find my true beauty. I had to embrace it, marks and all. I learned during this season that people didn't see what I saw. I focused on my imperfections and the enemy magnified those flaws. My marks and blemishes were not as bad as I thought, and over time not as important as I made them seem.

This season of discovery taught me a lot about myself and helped me to focus on more than just external blemishes. It was a cleansing time for me internally. I spent a great deal of time reading my Bible and truly developing a personal relationship with God. Much of what you read in this section will cover what I learned during and after this season of discovery. The following poem provides a greater understanding of this journey.

The Mirror

I had a seat in front of a mirror but didn't like what I see, for it wasn't a reflection of the outer, but my inner me.

Although my nails were polished and not a hair was out of place, The reflection went past the beaming eye's and the smile on my face.

This mirror's reflection was quit painful to see, for as much as I worked and worked there was still more to be worked out in me.

Things that I thought I conquered, fears that I thought I faced, were looking back at me like I was just beginning my race.

Those voices once silent began to scream loud, and they were no longer the voice of one but grew into a crowd.

Each one prancing by gloating on what they'd done, since they were a reflection of a battle I thought I'd won.

First came fear and not far behind was pride, then like two twins a reflection of envy and jealousy standing side by side.

Oh, what a reflection, what a sad sight to see that my enemies weren't on the outside but reflecting from inside of me.

But there was also a reflection that boldly stood in place, it was the Holy Spirit shining forth mercy and grace.

As I shifted my gaze and began to focus on Him, the crowd became silent and the images were dim.

I acknowledged to Him the issues which flowed out of my heart. In the midst of my confession the crowd had no choice but to part.

For the glory of the Lord began to flood each and every space, where the enemy tried to detour me and kick me out the race.

He invaded every chamber, he came rushing through every door, those that were prancing were now lying on the floor.

Out bitterness, out unforgiveness, I see you hurt trying to hide, out shame, out anger you can no longer abide.

They were evicted by His power, they were kicked out to return no more, for He is now the guard that sits at my hearts door.

I'm sitting in front of a mirror and all I want to see, is the heart of my Savior Jesus reflecting back at me.

In addition to sharing some of my personal experiences, I will also illustrate the applications of the different skin types we learned about in the previous section through a study of several women in the Bible.

The Bible is filled with beauty secrets and advice. In the next few chapters, we will discover women from years ago who had the same skin types we have today. We may not be able to determine their natural skin type; however, we will explore their spiritual skin type by looking at their particular situations and circumstances. Their stories will give us clarity and understanding of where we are spiritually. We will also see the effect of the different skin types and how the women coped with obstacles. Some of them were able to change their skin type while others did not. I pray their stories will inspire you to continue on your journey.

I remember years ago when an acquaintance of my father had a delicious looking white coconut cake. It was about six layers of milky white icing with coconut pieces. My father asked for the cake, but the woman didn't want to give it away at first. Eventually, she let him have it. When we got home all six of us were ready with our plates in hand. We watched my father take the knife and expose all six layers with icing seeping in between. It looked absolutely delicious. As we each took a bite, we were all caught by surprise; the way it looked and the way it tasted were two different things. It was hard to believe that something so beautiful had no flavor, and was tasteless and bland. Looking at the cake made our mouth water; eating it made us want to spit it out. We were quite disappointed.

Spiritually, we do not want to be like that cake. We don't want our outside to be so together, but have no substance, depth or beauty within. We don't want to be just a picture, one dimensional, or shallow.

46

We are made of three parts: soul, spirit and body. We want all three parts to have flavor.

Chapter 6

Do you Know Me?

We interact with people all the time. Some are perfect strangers, while others are family, co-workers and friends. But do we really know the people we come in contact with every day? I have evaluated some of my relationships, and I have come to the conclusion that some people really don't know me or my character. Their responses and reactions to me were a clear indication. This thought process led me to write the following poem.

Do you Know ME?
Do you know my value?
Do you know my worth?
What is means to step to my turf?
Do you know my wants?
Do you know my dreams what it takes to make my eye's beam?
Do you know my strength?
Do you know my fears?
What it takes to make my eye's swell up in tears?
Do you know my laughter?
Do you know my smile?
What I think makes life worthwhile?
Do you know my soul?
Do you know my mind?
What I do when I unwind?
Do you know my potential?
Do you know my past?
What it takes to make my love last?

Do you know my fire?

Do you know my drive?

The goals for which I strive?

Do you know my future?

Do you know my today?

The prices I have had to pay?

With all of these questions, as strange as they may be, ask yourself: Do you really know Me?

Questions often open the door to possibilities, direction and unlocking dreams. I originally presented this poem to others, but then it dawned on me: Do I know the answers to all of these questions? Do *I* really know me? I am still changing some answers and looking to fill in the blanks for others. Although we may not be able to answer all these questions, there's someone who knows the answers to these questions and many more. That person is our heavenly Father. What's so beautiful is that God wants to answer these questions for us. He doesn't want us to be unclear or in the dark.

It may take some time for you to answer all of the questions presented in this poem. Some questions are easy while others will take some time and reflection to come up with a proper response to discover the truth. Due to the influence of others, some answers will be difficult because the initial answers are not genuinely our own. Unfortunately, many of us have allowed other people to impose their thoughts and views on us to the point where it's difficult to know if the response is ours or derived from someone else's influence. It will take time to peel away the layers and reveal our own skin, but don't worry—you are worth the process!

In the movie *The Runaway Bride*, the lead female character adapted to the likes of every man she had a relationship with to the point where she didn't even know what type of eggs she liked. In one particular scene, she had a variety of egg dishes: scrambled, sunny side up, over easy, etc. She was trying to figure out which eggs she personally liked. This is a reflection of some of us. We have to take the time to become familiar with our own taste buds so we can discover what we really like and not what others have deemed acceptable. I'm not saying we shouldn't have influential people in our life, we should. The problem comes when we allow their influence to override who we are. We have our own mind, thoughts and opinions. They are to be valued, appreciated and respected.

Sadly many of us don't know our true identity. Many people find it easier to simply "blend in" in order to be accepted by others, instead of choosing to be the unique individual they were created to be. This is not the case for everyone, but I'll admit at different stages in my life this was the case for me. I've come to love being tall, but early in life I despised my height because I could never hide. I had my growth spurt in elementary school and stood several inches higher than even my teachers. I stood out even when I didn't want to. I had to ask myself: why do I want to hide? Why do I want to fit in? Why don't I want to stand out? This was during the time when I was truly spiritually oily. The insecurity and low self-esteem had oils pouring out of me in every direction. You may have similar issues. It may not be with height, but with another aspect of your being. The biblical account below shows us that standing out is not always a bad thing.

In the book of John we read about the woman at the well. In this powerful story we learn that she was no ordinary woman, but an oily skinned woman of controversy. She'd been married at least five times, and it's unclear exactly how many men she had actually been with. Many of us would not understand why Jesus would choose such a woman to break the strongholds of culture, race and religion. Let's take a deeper look at the scriptures.

He left Judaea, and departed again into Galilee. And he must needs go through Samaria.

-- John 4:3-4

Jesus was doing a work, when there arose an urgency for Him to go through Samaria. The term *must needs* conveys that He was not going for leisure, but for something important. One translation states it was "necessary" for Him to go. There was a purpose and mission prompting Him to go through that particular city.

Then cometh he to a city of Samaria, which is called Sychar, near to the parcel of ground that Jacob gave to his son Joseph. Now Jacob's well was there. Jesus therefore, being wearied with his journey, sat thus on the well: and it was about the sixth hour. There cometh a woman of Samaria to draw water: Jesus saith unto her, Give me to drink.

-- John 4:5-7

The verse states that Jesus arrived at the well at the sixth hour, which is noon. In biblical times the women went to draw from wells early to avoid the hot sun. Since this task was performed daily around the same time, the women probably worked and traveled in groups. However, in this passage we read that when this woman came to the well in the heat of the day, she came alone. This symbolizes to us that she was an outcast; and just as people avoided her, she wanted to avoid them.

Not only did Jesus show up at the well, He also addressed her directly and asked her a question. I'm sure with her history, she was not used to a man asking her a question that was not degrading. The fact that He said anything to her probably shocked her because it wasn't Jewish custom for a Jew to talk to a Samaritan. Jesus speaking to her knowing her ethnicity probably caught her off guard. This could be seen as the equivalent of a prince talking to a prostitute. It was not an acceptable association.

Then saith the woman of Samaria unto him, How is it that thou, being a Jew, askest drink of me, which am a woman of Samaria? for the Jews have no dealings with the Samaritans.

-- John 4:9

The woman identified Jesus as a Jew and did not expect that He would want to communicate with her. At some point many of us may have felt this way. We may have felt Jesus wanted nothing to do with us because of our oily skin and the sin in our life. However, just as Jesus met the woman at the well, He also stands at the well of your soul. Just as her background, ethnicity and past did not hinder Him from coming to her, our past does not hinder Him from coming to us.

At this, Jesus said to her, Go, call your husband and come back here. The woman answered, I have no husband. Jesus said to her, You have spoken truly in saying, I have no husband. For you have had five husbands, and the man you are now living with is not your husband. In this you have spoken truly.

-- John 9:16-18

There is much to learn from the verses above. Again, we have two people whose cultures did not permit open communication, yet they continued to engage each other. Jesus offered her something and did not ask for anything in return, which intrigued the woman. She was blown away to say the least. When Jesus shifted the focus on her, the woman did what many of us with oily skin often fail to do: she was honest. She probably felt relieved to finally be able to freely tell the truth. She may have wanted to change her life for a while, but didn't know how. She probably wanted a fresh start, but didn't know where to go. Jesus, a stranger, asked her a question, which began her quest to freedom.

I have adopted a rule: I don't lie to myself; therefore, I don't lie to others. I used to lie to myself. I was not honest about my feelings, thoughts or emotions. I was trying to please people and that left me miserable. I could no longer function. When I surrendered and made Jesus my Lord and Savior, He began to show, cultivate and mold me into the unique individual He created me to be. I had to dispose of a plethora of emotional baggage. Jesus had to break old mindsets and attitudes. He began to fashion me into His image. This is an ever-evolving process.

Do you want to trade in your oily skin?

Are you tired of carrying the weight of sin?

Are you ready to release the baggage of your past?

Are you tired of the shame and the embarrassment?

Are you tired of lying to yourself and to others?

Do you want to be free to breathe again?

If you answered yes to any of the above questions, today could be your day of change and freedom.

When Jesus met the woman at the well, she was open and receptive to him. Most importantly, she was honest with herself first, then with Jesus. She listened to Him recite her past. She did not lie when the truth about her was revealed. Jesus recalled the past, not to expose the woman, but to acknowledge her honesty.

We must do the same. When the truth about where we are and where we have been surfaces, we must take ownership. Lying will perpetuate a vicious cycle of sin. Being honest will set us free. The questions Jesus posed went beneath the surface. The woman was probably familiar with men speaking about her natural beauty; however, Jesus dealt with her spiritual beauty. Some of us are praised for what we wear on the outside, but internally we are crying out for someone to hear our heart. Jesus is waiting patiently to dig beneath the surface and heal our brokenness. Only then can we truly enjoy freedom.

Then the woman left her water jar and went away to the town. And she began telling the people, Come, see a Man Who has told me everything that I ever did!

--John 4:28-29

54

When we experience freedom, we want to share the news with everyone. Here we meet a woman who simply went to draw water by herself in the day. She was considered an outcast, but after talking with Jesus, the woman ran back to the town and told everyone. In one conversation she was healed, delivered and set free. In one conversation, she was given hope, peace and encouragement. In one conversation, her burdens were lifted and pain was replaced with joy. The woman was so excited that she went to the same people who had talked about her, rejected her and made her feel ashamed; she didn't care about the possible backlash. She was so liberated it did not matter. Her testimony was so strong and powerful that men came looking for Jesus. One talk with Jesus transformed her skin from oily to normal. We can apply her actions to our life.

There comes a time in life when questions are necessary. Children find answers by asking questions. Somewhere between childhood and adulthood this propensity dissipates, possibly because we don't want to know the truth or deal with reality. I came to this point in my early twenties after graduating from college. I was employed with a really good company but, due management's lack of integrity, I lost the job. This caused me to ask, "What do I really want to do?" "What are my passions?" "What job would I do for free?" "What do I see for my future?" "Why am I here?" Many times it takes a loss for us to start looking for our value and purpose.

In order to benefit from the concepts in this book, we must make ourselves a priority. Some of us have never done this. We have been there for everyone but ourselves. We must take care of ourselves in order to be beneficial to others. Making ourselves a priority is not pride. Not caring for ourselves is false humility, which is a form of pride. I've watched women pour their all on others and leave nothing for themselves. We need balance. It's like a chef who cooks meals for others, but is always hungry and dying from malnutrition. The chef has access to food yet doesn't eat. Does that make any sense? No. Neither does not making ourselves a priority.

False humility is a form of bondage. It makes us feel worthless, unappreciated and of no value. It keeps us bound with low self-perception and low self-esteem. These false realties are lies from the enemy. We learn our value and worth from the One who created us, through His Word. We can be so enthralled with performing activities that we never stop or even think to ask God, "Why Am I here?" Some of us are on the path to purpose, but are we reaching our full potential? Many of us are like a letter that keeps going to the wrong location; we're loaded with return stickers. We keep trying to get to the correct location, but each place we get to, they stamp us "return to sender." And we search again and, just when we think we've arrived, instead of being accepted, they pull out that ink stamp and return us again.

As a journalism major, I love to ask questions. In order to have a clear picture of where we are, where we have been and where we want to go, we *must* ask questions. Not only must we ask the hard questions, we also need to be honest with our responses. As you do the following exercise, take some time to really think before you answer. Pray about it and see what God has to say. Then write down your thoughts in the space provided. Take this time to really analyze who you are.

Do you know yourself?

_____

_____

_____

_____

_____

_____

_____

_____

Do you like what you see?

_____

_____

_____

_____

_____

_____

_____

_____

Does your perception line up with His will?

_____

_____

_____

_____

_____

_____

_____

_____

_____

If you could make changes, what would you remove, minimize or enhance?

_____

_____

_____

_____

_____

_____

_____

_____

Prayer

Father I thank You that You love me in spite of my shortcomings and imperfections. I thank You that Your plans for me are beyond anything I could ever think of or imagine. I thank You that I can be completely honest with You and that You won't judge me in my honesty. Like the woman at the well, I will respond properly as You share with me. I am willing to make the necessary changes to come into complete alignment with Your will and purpose for my life. Open my eyes that I may see like I've never seen before, and not only see, but believe. In Jesus name, Amen.

Chapter 7
Are You a Fragrance or an Odor?

*H*ave you ever walked in a room and asked, "What is that smell?" This question could come from a positive or negative position. When I worked as a makeup artist in a department store, I was often stationed near the fragrance department. On some days there would be so many different scents in the air that you would almost choke. Even with such an array of perfumes, there were odors that would override the fragrances.

Finding the perfect fragrance is a hunt I have been on for some years now. When you find that perfect fragrance, it exudes out of you all day long. It just seems to blend with the natural oils of your skin. I personally know of people who have found their signature scent. There is no denying the perfect fragrance. It is disappointing when a perfume smells great, but when you wear it no one can smell it on you… then after a while you can't even smell it. The right fragrance makes a world of difference.

Smells have their own type of power. They can get your attention without your permission and sometimes even hold you captive. I've actually smelled some people before I saw them; sometimes it was a good thing and other times, not so good. The smell that exudes from a person may come from something on the surface or from an internal source. One should know whether what they exude is a fragrance or an odor.

The story of Esther is a great example of the beautification process. There are many truths that we can learn, as well as see the benefits of investing our time wisely. Through her story we learn that one's background or circumstances doesn't determine what spiritual skin type one will have. Esther was orphaned and raised by an uncle. That alone could have made her spiritually sensitive or dry, but it didn't. Esther's normal skin was comprised of humility and obedience.

Let the king appoint commissioners in every province of his realm to bring all these beautiful young women into the harem at the citadel of Susa. Let them be placed under the care of Hegai, the king's eunuch, who is in charge of the women; and let beauty treatments be given to them. ⁴ Then let the young woman who pleases the king be queen instead of Vashti." This advice appealed to the king, and he followed it.⁵ Now there was in the citadel of Susa a Jew of the tribe of Benjamin, named Mordecai son of Jair, the son of Shimei, the son of Kish, ⁶ who had been carried into exile from Jerusalem by Nebuchadnezzar king of Babylon, among those taken captive with Jehoiachin king of Judah. ⁷ Mordecai had a cousin named Hadassah, whom he had brought up because she had neither father nor mother. This young woman, who was also known as Esther, had a lovely figure and was beautiful. Mordecai had taken her as his own daughter when her father and mother died.

--Esther 2:3-7 NIV

By this time the king had banished the former queen and was looking for someone to replace her. Now this was not an easy task to fulfill. These young virgins weren't going to the palace for a field trip. They were going to endure the preparation process, after which they would seek to find favor in the king's sight. This is a rare scripture; it actually describes Esther's external appearance. It is said that she had a lovely figure and was beautiful, truly a description we rarely see in scripture. We also learn she was orphaned.

[8] When the king's order and edict had been proclaimed, many young women were brought to the citadel of Susa and put under the care of Hegai. Esther also was taken to the king's palace and entrusted to Hegai, who had charge of the harem. [9] She pleased him and won his favor. Immediately he provided her with her beauty treatments and special food. He assigned to her seven female attendants selected from the king's palace and moved her and her attendants into the best place in the harem.

-- Esther 2:8-9 NIV

These verses speak of how well Mordecai had raised Esther. Although she went into the palace, Esther's character was not formed in the palace. There were some attributes and qualities she had before she crossed the threshold of the palace. It was those attributes and qualities that caused her to be favored.

Many of us will be used in palace-like environments. The challenge is obtaining the qualifications before we get there. Some things cannot be learned on the job. The key is preparation. Esther was already prepared spiritually; the purification process was for natural purposes. She already exuded a fragrance even before she started the treatments, and Hegai (who had charge of the women) could smell it. Think of the multitude of young women in that harem; clearly it had to take more than physical beauty to catch Hegai's eye.

¹² Before a young woman's turn came to go in to King Xerxes, she had to complete twelve months of beauty treatments prescribed for the women, six months with oil of myrrh and six with perfumes and cosmetics.

-- Esther 2:12 NIV

I find it very interesting that the women chosen were virgins, yet they weren't pure enough for the king. They were not just being washed, they were being purified. Purification is removing all toxins and impurities out of our system, re-establishing balance, and adding the essential properties to keep our bodies properly aligned. When we become spiritually purified, sin is removed from our lives through Christ and replaced with the Word of God, which is also His will. This is a continual process.

Many times we like the end result, yet we want to skip the process it takes to get there. I remember one year I flew home for Thanksgiving. My flight was so late that by the time I arrived, the food was prepped, cooked and put away. I didn't have to cut or slice vegetables or prep any food. I just fixed a plate. Likewise, many of us want to fix a spiritual plate, but the process doesn't work that way. We have to go through purification.

¹³ And this is how she would go to the king: Anything she wanted was given her to take with her from the harem to the king's palace. ¹⁴ In the evening she would go there and in the morning return to another part of the harem to the care of Shaashgaz, the king's eunuch who was in charge of the concubines. She would not return to the king unless he was pleased with her and summoned her by name.

-- Esther 2:13-14 NIV

I must make mention of the fact that the young women were given whatever they desired. We can only imagine how much or how little some of the women took. Just think, what if you were in a competition to become the First Lady of the United States? Upon completing the required beauty treatments, you are then given a black credit card to Saks 5th Avenue in New York City to purchase whatever you wanted for your meeting with the president. What would you purchase? Jewelry? Would you buy a whole wardrobe in preparation of being selected? Would you get just one outfit? Think on that for a moment and be honest.

15 When the turn came for Esther (the young woman Mordecai had adopted, the daughter of his uncle Abihail) to go to the king, she asked for nothing other than what Hegai, the king's eunuch who was in charge of the harem, suggested. And Esther won the favor of everyone who saw her. 16 She was taken to King Xerxes in the royal residence in the tenth month, the month of Tebeth, in the seventh year of his reign.

-- Esther2:15-16 NIV

There are two major points I want to address. The first is that Esther had patience. She was not taken to the king first. We do not know her position in the line, but time had passed and she did not grow impatient. Many of us become impatient at the wrong time. We must soak in the oils and perfumes until God says it's time. The second point is that she required nothing aside from what was suggested by Hegai. She was humble and had wisdom. I believe Esther understood it was not about her, but about the king. She did not come with selfish motives; she came with a humble spirit and a submitted heart. She was about to worship the natural king the way we should worship our spiritual King. This is what worship is: surrendering our all to please God.

[17] Now the king was attracted to Esther more than to any of the other women, and she won his favor and approval more than any of the other virgins. So he set a royal crown on her head and made her queen instead of Vashti.

-- Esther 2:17 NIV

We all have battles great and small. Esther had a battle, although we don't read about it. It must have been difficult growing up without her parents. It also seems as if she had no siblings and was moved to an unfamiliar place. All of this had to be taxing on the young woman. And like Esther, we have been challenged in some way, shape or form. We have to make a decision to deal with the challenges and no longer stand on the sidelines or sit in the outfield. We have to get up, brush ourselves off, and get moving. We have to make a decision - through the challenge, will we become better or bitter? If we choose better, some issues that seem huge will begin to shrink as our focus and perspective shifts.

Esther's beauty treatments imbued her with fragrances. While she soaked in them, the fragrances seeped into her skin and thereafter they exuded from her. When we allow the Word of God to rest in our spirit, the Word will flow from our lips and release into the atmosphere and into the ears of others. We can tell a lot about a person by what they say. We learn from the Bible that out of the mouth flow the issues of the heart. If you want to identify your issues, listen to your conversations. Then you will know what you need to work on.

We cannot conquer anything we won't acknowledge. Therefore, the first thing we must do is acknowledge our issues. In the process, we often learn that we first need to forgive ourselves. When we free ourselves from the bondage of unforgiveness, we can release and forgive others.

Internal beautification transforms our heart. When the heart is pure, everything else will be pure.

The fragrances of patience, submission, humility, wisdom and obedience are cultivated with time. Some will emit and emanate from us quicker than others. Some of us have an odor of fear, insecurity, hate, anger, bitterness, rejection and lust permeating from us. As we beautify the inside, our scent will change to a lovely fragrance. We should then begin to associate with others who are exuding the same fragrance. The fragrance begins from the mouth, the words you speak, and as it is absorbed deeper into your spirit, it begins to exude from your actions and attitude.

Upon entering a room full of people we can smell a variety of scents, from perfume to cigarette smoke. It is the same with people's words. We can hear bitterness, anger, hate, envy and jealousy. Sometimes we see those traits through mannerisms. Many non-smokers do not appreciate the smell of smoke. The problem with being in close contact with a smoker is that the residue lingers. You can try to cover up the smell with perfume and cologne, but the scent clings to your hair and clothes. It is the same thing with anger, hatred and bitterness. We can try to cover it with a smile or laugh, but it does not take long for it to permeate from our mouths and linger.

I don't know about you, but its challenging to be around a negative person. They seem to never see the positive side of anything. Negative people need much healing and a real encounter with the true love of God. The constant negativity is a reflection of an internal struggle. I've witnessed several beautiful occasions become tainted by negativity. I watched a show on TV about brides trying to find the perfect wedding dress. It was amazing to see how negative some of the moms and siblings were on such an important occasion. Some of the brides were called fat, ugly and huge. Can you imagine hearing that while trying on your wedding gown? It was appalling to hear and watch. The words spoken were so odorous and offensive.

Speaking words that are nasty, evil, hurtful, and judgmental and condemning will carry a foul odor. It's like having morning breath all day. This is not what we want others to see or smell when they hear us. The Bible speaks of sweet words:

Pleasant words are as a honeycomb, sweet to the soul, and health to the bones.

-- Proverbs 16:24

I once knew a man who, from the outside, everything seemed fine, but when he opened his mouth, his teeth were beyond yellow. They had gook on them like he never brushed. You could see it in the gums. It looked like he always ate popcorn and the popcorn kept getting stuck in his gums. Do you know how unattractive that looks? I won't even mention the smell. For some of us, this is how our words look and affect other people. Just as his teeth were a negative reflection of him, our words can be a negative reflection of us.

I am not a farmer and I don't know much about agriculture, but I do know the difference between an apple and an orange. I can also look at some fruit and see if it is unripe, ripe or rotten. With some fruit, you can't tell from the outside what condition it's in, but when you take a bite, you are instantly aware of its true state. Likewise, some people cannot tell who we are by the way we dress, what we drive or where we work. But when we open our mouth and speak, they can see if we are unripe, ripe or rotten. There is so much revealed about us by the words we speak!

The other issue is what scents are the people around us permeating? If you were in a car with a smoker then afterward you both walk into a building, it would be hard to determine who the actual smoker is. Because of the company we keep, some of us are permeating scents that are not even ours. People may think we are angry, mean or stuck up because of who we surround ourselves with. How many people are avoiding us because of smells that don't belong to us? We all need to take a sniff test to see if we are carrying someone else's fragrance or odor.

The story of Esther depicts someone with a fragrance, not an odor. Her obedience, humility and wisdom caused the crown to be set upon her head. She was balanced; she knew how to carry and conduct herself. She had queenly virtues. Esther's qualities were embedded in her before she arrived at the palace. How will your story end? Will you be adequately prepared when the Lord calls you to your palace?

Prayer

Father cause me to embrace my process. Let me not allow pride or haughtiness to stop me from receiving truth from You or others. I willingly step into a season of beautification from the inside out. Cause me to be sensitive to that which I speak about others and the thoughts I even have about myself. I receive the challenge of beautification and will seep myself for as long as it takes. Show me the odorous and offensive words I've released and help me to understand why. May I no longer harbor jealousy, envy, pride, low self-esteem or fear. But let a new confidence, which comes from You, begin to rise in me and flow out of me. May I truly become a new creature in Christ during this season.

Chapter 8
Who & Why?

If "we" do not set standards for ourselves, none will be set. Without established rules, there is no order. If we don't set parameters, we allow complete lack of control. We place ourselves in positions of powerlessness, permitting others to treat us however they want, whenever they want. Many people fear setting priorities, standards and parameters with their emotions and in their relationships, as if it is improper for them to do. However, such restrictions are necessary if we want healthy relationships with ourselves and others.

Imagine a neighborhood without boundary regulations. How would each lot size be determined? What roads would be paved? Where would the street lights be placed? Who would make those decisions? Each land owner? Can you imagine how disproportionate that neighborhood would look? Webster's defines a boundary as "something that indicates or fixes a limit or extent." If there were no boundaries in a neighborhood, one neighbor could end up building a mansion while others were only left with enough land to build a hut. One house may have an Olympic sized pool while another barely has room for a tub. Where there is no structure, people tend to take advantage.

This same logic holds true in our emotional lives. If we do not have our own set of values, a more dominant person can control or take advantage of us. There are those of us who have always been unprotected, open and exposed. Some of us had boundaries that were beaten down by the storms of life. In both cases, in order to create a space for our future growth and nourishment, these boundaries need to be rebuilt. But that begs the question - how many safeguards are needed to protect our spiritual skin type?

Most of us know how a bank account works. To open a new account, a minimum balance is usually required. In order to pay minimal or no fees, some financial institutions require a direct deposit be made into the account on a regular basis. For example, they may require that you register a payroll check to ensure that money is placed in the account each month. The bank generally issues a bank card, which you can use to make purchases and withdrawals, which draws funds directly from your account. You may also be allowed to set up automatic debits and transfers from your account that withdraw funds on a schedule you determine. The ability to use several methods to input or withdraw funds causes the balance to change constantly. Therefore, banks have introduced technology that enables us to check our account balances using a smartphone or computer. Some banks even send email alerts or text messages to let you know your balance is low. Use of technology is critical since your bank can charge overdraft fees.

I adopted this banking concept in relationships with associates, friends and family. Whatever initially attracted us or caused us to enter into a relationship of any kind is the minimum balance for that relationship. Perhaps there was something done or said that made us comfortable connecting with the person. As we talk and spend time together, direct deposits are added to the original balance, or debits and transfers are subtracted. These transactions are positive or negative expenditures of our emotions, time and energy. People who consistently drain you emotionally, those who are always needy, are like scheduled debits or transfers from your balance. People who bring drama or negativity are like bank card purchases or withdrawals. Individuals who are consistently encouraging and motivating are like payroll checks, regularly adding to your emotional account. If you are able to maintain a positive relationship account balance, continue in the relationship as it is adding value to your life. Oftentimes, the problem is in determining whether a relationship balance is low and can be replenished with a credit in the future, or if the account is overdrawn.

Relationships, like bank accounts, begin at varying levels. Some of our relationship accounts were established with high balances that have grown even higher due to steady deposits. Other accounts had very little to start with. There were minimal deposits in the form of good communication for a few weeks, then the relationship shifted as the person was no longer available to answer our calls. If an individual chooses to close the account, do not force the issue. Consider that transaction complete and move on. When we try to hold open a relationship account with a negative balance, we suffer, just as holding open an overdrawn bank account causes us to accrue continual fees. We jeopardize our financial condition and accounts when we attempt to withdraw from them and insist on keeping the overdrawn account open. The same is true for emotional accounts. When we continue to attempt to withdraw from negative relationships that are already overdrawn, it is detrimental to our overall emotional and spiritual well-being.

I have a phrase that I use: *I'm in a place.* During this time of quietness, I ask the questions: Who and why? Sometimes we get so caught up in new areas and seasons of our life, that we do not assess who is in our life and why they are there. During this time, I talk to a selected group of people. I read my Bible and spend a lot of time in prayer. It can last for a day, or for weeks depending upon what I need and when I receive clarity. It's a time of assessment for me.

I must admit it took a lot for me to gain control over of my emotions and my relationship accounts. I had to change my phone number a few times, but it helped me to disengage from negative relationships. I was hesitant initially about changing my number, just like I would hesitate to change banks in order to eliminate bad accounts. Then, someone from one of my positive relationships stated, "There are too many people taking from you. Friends are supposed to deposit, not take." That motivated me to take action. I began deleting numbers, in an effort to rid myself of negative accounts. Then, I heard a still small voice say, "They can still call you." That really made me re-evaluate who and why. Who have I allowed in my life and why are they there? Are they a benefit? Is there value? Are they a crediting or a debiting relationship? After this thorough evaluation, I changed my number, but I was finally okay. I've repeated this action of evaluation in different seasons of my life.

Do you check your bank account to see what you have been charged for and to make sure there are not charges that should not be there? If you can reconcile your bank account, you can reconcile your emotional account. A silent moment with God clears our mind and allows us to hear God's will for our life. When we understand what God's will is, we view things and people with a new perspective. Just as we can find incorrect charges on our bank account, we may find out someone is not a true friend. Or, just like we find overcharges, we may find that someone we thought was a friend is actually an associate or a co-worker; nothing more, nothing less. I cannot tell you how often you should check your emotional account, but I can say that if you are in a season of transition, this is a good time for a thorough inspection. If you are in the midst of making a life-changing decision, now is a good time. If there is a lot of confusion in your life and little or no peace, an emotional account check is in order.

You would be surprised how incorrect our emotional account statements can be. How many weights and burdens we carry that are not even ours. There is a liberation that comes with reconciling your account that is indescribable. When you try it you will understand. I highly encourage you to ask "Who and why?" You may encounter resistance, even fear and guilt; however, you must do what is best for your emotional balance. I'm not saying become a hermit, but be wise. Your mind, heart and spirit will thank you.

The story of Abigail in 1 Samuel makes one wonder how a woman with queenly qualities could marry such a fool? During Old Testament times many women were unable to choose who they married. Most marriages were arranged to position families for wealth, stability and social status. This custom is still practiced in some cultures. It is possible Abigail may have despised the arrangement, but did not have much choice. Still, her story shows us an example of combination skin.

2 A certain man in Maon, who had property there at Carmel, was very wealthy. He had a thousand goats and three thousand sheep, which he was shearing in Carmel. 3 His name was Nabal and his wife's name was Abigail. She was an intelligent and beautiful woman, but her husband was surly and mean in his dealings—he was a Calebite.

--1 Samuel 25:2-3 NIV

Although Abigail had good qualities, her environment caused her to have issues. As I stated earlier, we must not only know our skin type, we must also consider our environment and season. Have you ever seen a couple and wondered: *how in the world did they end up together?* I'm sure some people felt the same way about Abigail and Nabal. Just look how they are described. One Bible translation describes Abigail as a woman of good understanding, which means she had wisdom, knowledge and intellect. Abigail's character shows she had an account in good standing; however, you can see from her husband's description that he withdrew a lot from her account. With those favorable qualities, why would Abigail develop combination skin? Her environment caused her skin issues.

Her husband is described as evil, rough and a Calebite; he was not a nice man. Have you ever met a man who was just plain mean and his wife or girlfriend was just as sweet as she could be? It's a strange combination. The Scripture does not say, but many times when a man is domineering, he is also abusive. As the story continues, David asked Nabal for a favor.

[4] While David was in the wilderness, he heard that Nabal was shearing sheep. [5] So he sent ten young men and said to them, "Go up to Nabal at Carmel and greet him in my name. [6] Say to him: 'Long life to you! Good health to you and your household! And good health to all that is yours!' [7] "Now I hear that it is sheep-shearing time. When your shepherds were with us, we did not mistreat them, and the whole time they were at Carmel nothing of theirs was missing. [8] Ask your own servants and they will tell you. Therefore be favorable toward my men, since we come at a festive time. Please give your servants and your son David whatever you

can find for them.'"[9] When David's men arrived, they gave Nabal this message in David's name. Then they waited.

--1 Samuel 25:4-9

David was respectable with his petition to Nabal. Before asking for anything, David blessed him. Have you ever seen someone just snap at another person for absolutely no reason? They assume the whole world is against them. It is hard to deal with an angry and bitter woman, but as we find in Nabal's response, an angry man is worse.

[10] Nabal answered David's servants, "Who is this David? Who is this son of Jesse? Many servants are breaking away from their masters these days. [11] Why should I take my bread and water, and the meat I have slaughtered for my shearers, and give it to men coming from who knows where?"[12] David's men turned around and went back. When they arrived, they reported every word.

--1 Samuel 25:10-12 NIV

David was the captain of an army, not some "nobody" asking around for a favor. He was a commanding officer—a man of great stature, who would be able to repay Nabal for his goods and services. David was the one who fought on his behalf, which allowed him to keep the wealth that he had acquired. But Nabal responded like a fool. This can be likened to when you see people cursing out a judge or a teacher. They have no respect for authority. These officials are here to serve and protect us.

[13] David said to his men, "Each of you strap on your sword!" So they did, and David strapped his on as well. About four hundred men went up with David, while two hundred stayed with the supplies. [14] One of the servants told Abigail, Nabal's wife, "David sent messengers from the wilderness to give our master his greetings, but he hurled insults at them. [15] Yet these men were very good to us. They did not mistreat us, and the whole time we were out in the fields near them nothing was missing. [16] Night and day they were a wall around us the whole time we were herding our sheep near them. [17] Now think it over and see what you can do, because disaster is hanging over our master and his whole household. He is such a wicked man that no one can talk to him."

--1 Samuel 25: 13-17 NIV

In the end, Nabal's foolishness destroyed him. His account had a negative balance. How many of us have lost money, sleep and peace dealing with people who function like Nabal? How many of us have lost or almost lost what we had on account of our environment? This is how our skin becomes oily. Some people need to change not only their skin treatment but also their social environment altogether.

[18] Abigail acted quickly. She took two hundred loaves of bread, two skins of wine, five dressed sheep, five seahs of roasted grain, a hundred cakes of raisins and two hundred cakes of pressed figs, and loaded them on donkeys. [19] Then she told her servants, "Go on ahead; I'll follow you." But she did not tell her husband Nabal. [20] As she came riding her donkey into a mountain ravine, there were David and his men descending toward her, and she met them.

--1 Samuel 25:18-20 NIV

Although Nabal was foolish, Abigail was a woman of means who knew what to do. She was also a woman of influence. We need to be more like Abigail. If people in our environment do not care about their own lives, we have to want to live enough for ourselves. For some this may mean ending relationships. I would rather end a relationship than lose my life by staying in one that is deadly. If it is a severely difficult situation, possibly life threatening, then we must pray for wisdom because every issue cannot be handled in the same manner. If we ask God, He will tell us what to do and how to do it.

Abigail moved with haste. She didn't wait for disaster to strike; she went to it. Some situations can be handled effectively if we react and move swiftly. Abigail was bold and purposed to do what was best despite Nabal's foolishness.

[23] When Abigail saw David, she quickly got off her donkey and bowed down before David with her face to the ground. [24] She fell at his feet and said: "Pardon your servant, my lord, and let me speak to you; hear what your servant has to say. [25] Please pay no attention, my lord, to that wicked man Nabal. He is just like his name—his name means Fool, and folly goes with him. And as for me, your servant, I did not see the men my lord sent. [26] And now, my lord, as surely as the Lord your God lives and as you live, since the Lord has kept you from bloodshed and from avenging yourself with your own hands, may your enemies and all who are intent on harming my lord be like Nabal. [27] And let this gift, which your servant has brought to my lord, be given to the men who follow you. [28] "Please forgive your servant's presumption. The Lord your God will certainly make a lasting dynasty for my lord, because you fight the Lord's battles, and no wrongdoing will be found in you as long as you

live. ²⁹ Even though someone is pursuing you to take your life, the life of my lord will be bound securely in the bundle of the living by the Lord your God, but the lives of your enemies he will hurl away as from the pocket of a sling. ³⁰ When the Lord has fulfilled for my lord every good thing he promised concerning him and has appointed him ruler over Israel, ³¹ my lord will not have on his conscience the staggering burden of needless bloodshed or of having avenged himself. And when the Lord your God has brought my lord success, remember your servant."³² David said to Abigail, "Praise be to the Lord, the God of Israel, who has sent you today to meet me. ³³ May you be blessed for your good judgment and for keeping me from bloodshed this day and from avenging myself with my own hands. ³⁴ Otherwise, as surely as the Lord, the God of Israel, lives, who has kept me from harming you, if you had not come quickly to meet me, not one male belonging to Nabal would have been left alive by daybreak."³⁵ Then David accepted from her hand what she had brought him and said, "Go home in peace. I have heard your words and granted your request."

--1 Samuel 25:23-35 NIV

Abigail's petition averted her own destruction and the destruction of those she loved. Many of us need to learn how to speak when faced with adversity. She did not have a negative attitude or a proud disposition. Abigail was humble, and humility is a virtue we all should seek to obtain. She not only spoke well, she offered David wisdom, which he received. Many times it's not that people don't want to hear what we have to say, we just have to say it the right way. If you say something powerful with the wrong spirit, it will lose its potency. If we speak with humility, like Abigail, many of us will see things shift in our favor like it did for her.

^{38} About ten days later, the LORD struck Nabal and he died.^{39} ^{40b} "Then David sent word to Abigail, asking her to become his wife. ^{40} His servants went to Carmel and said to Abigail, "David has sent us to you to take you to become his wife."^{41} She bowed down with her face to the ground and said, "I am your servant and am ready to serve you and wash the feet of my lord's servants." ^{42} Abigail quickly got on a donkey and, attended by her five female servants, went with David's messengers and became his wife.

-- 1 Samuel 25: 38, 40-42

What a way to end a story! I'm sure Abigail was pained by the loss of her husband, yet honored to become the wife of a future king. A godly man was able to see her value and greatness and, when given the opportunity, he chose to marry and cherish her.

Now is a good time to take inventory. Look at all of the relationships you have: family, friends and associates. Can you honestly answer who and why? Are they adding to you or subtracting? Are they multiplying or causing division? Do you have a Nabal in your life? Have relationships caused your emotional bank account to be on the negative or the positive side? What does your spiritual bank account look like?

Prayer

Father I pray You help me take an honest assessment of the "who's & why's" in my life. Let me no longer avoid truth that has been shown to me. I pray for wisdom on how to handle the hard cases and the challenging conversations to come. But I will not allow fear to stop me from reconciling my emotional bank account. I chose to have an attitude of gratitude and learn from each person and situation. Order my steps to the new people and places that You would have for this season of my life.

Chapter 9

You're Waiting for Boaz but are you Ruth?

Waiting

Time feels like it slips away, another minute gone, another hour, another day, Waiting.

Dreams which seemed distant begin to flood my mind, for You are the author and finisher, You redeem the time, Waiting.

Sometimes I feel like I'm moving forward, while other times I feel like I'm standing still, but I've submitted to the process surrendering my soul, my mind, my will, Waiting.

Watching others begin to soar, watching others begin to leap, but I feel like I'm going up a hill that is very, very steep, Waiting.

Knowing I'm being strengthened, knowing I'm being made strong, knowing I will get to the place You've ordained all along, Waiting.

When the storms come to try and dim my light, when the enemy comes to steal my passion, zeal and fight, Waiting.

For I know there is a people, I know there is a time, I know You have the answer, I know there is a sign, Waiting.

I remain in a state of readiness, a patient enduring position, For Your prepared place comes with much increase and acquisition, Waiting.

I await the fulfillment of promise, I expect dreams come true, For I will not be made ashamed for my waiting is for You, Waiting.

While I wait I will worship, while I wait I will praise, while I wait in this posture I know I capture Your gaze, Waiting.

For my wait isn't misery, it's for purpose to be achieved. My waiting draws me closer to You, My heart longs for and cleaves, Waiting.

For You are downloading character and essential tools I will need, For You have much for me to do and many for me to feed, Waiting.

I smile and rest assured that my waiting is not in vain, For me to live is Christ and to die is gain, Waiting.

Waiting with great hope and expectation, waiting with great joy and anticipation, Waiting.

We live in a society that hates to wait on anything. I remember having to wait on the bus in Chicago's winters. That was not a pleasant experience. I stood in the blowing wind looking down the street hoping to see that blue CTA bus. Unfortunately, although it was scheduled, sometimes the bus did not come. I was left cold and frustrated—not a good combination. I believe waiting is a skill.

Some things that are worth waiting for are fruit to ripen, seasons to change, a graduation or the birth of a child. While waiting, there is an excitement and expectation that grows daily. When fulfillment comes, we value and appreciate the occasion even more. What do you think is worth the wait?

I have been asked many times why I'm not married. My response is, "I'm worth the wait." I don't want just anything or anybody. In the past, I've settled in relationships, but I refuse to settle now. I cannot settle with marriage; it is too important. The man I marry will determine my lifestyle. Lifestyle is not just where or how we live, but also our emotional, financial and physical well-being. I want God's best. I know my future husband will not be perfect; however, he will be a well-made man. I heard someone say, "Half a man is better than no man." My question is which half are you getting? You may only get half of him, but one-hundred percent of his drama and one-hundred percent of his issues!

Let's try to apply this thought process to other areas in our lives. Would you drive half a car? Would you live in half a house? Do we work for half a pay check? If you are putting in all that effort and energy, don't you want one hundred percent? You cannot make up the difference for what a person is lacking. Everything needs to be whole—including us. Two halves cannot make a whole when it comes to relationships. Two *whole* people make one whole relationship. On the journey to wholeness, sometimes you have to walk alone. You cannot be afraid to explore the dark places. They will soon become lit areas when you allow God to heal and restore you.

Many women prefer to work on others as a way to avoid working on themselves. How can you build something in someone else that you have not built in you? When you spend time working on yourself, it yields a great outcome that others can see, appreciate, and learn from.

Many unmarried women say they are waiting on Boaz, yet they have done nothing to prepare for him. Boaz may come, but are you Ruth? Have you left the familiar, that place of comfort? Are you willing to sacrifice for the betterment of others? Are you willing to leave all to follow the Lord? Are you submitted? Can you take instruction? Below we will read the account of Ruth and look at everything she did before Boaz appeared in her life.

Ruth is a great example of someone whose history did not determine her destiny. She was a Moabite, a pagan culture known for idol worship. They practiced perversion, harlotry and greed. This is the environment Ruth grew up in; however, this is not what she became. Although our surroundings can be oily, we don't have to be. In transitioning, we can keep our normal skin as we find a better climate. Ruth is an example of normal skin not influenced by the environment.

In the days when the judges ruled, there was a famine in the land. So a man from Bethlehem in Judah, together with his wife and two sons, went to live for a while in the country of Moab. [2] The man's name was

Elimelek, his wife's name was Naomi, and the names of his two sons were Mahlon and Kilion. They were Ephrathites from Bethlehem, Judah. And they went to Moab and lived there.³ Now Elimelek, Naomi's husband, died, and she was left with her two sons. ⁴ They married Moabite women, one named Orpah and the other Ruth. After they had lived there about ten years, ⁵ both Mahlon and Kilion also died, and Naomi was left without her two sons and her husband.

-- Ruth 1:1-5 NIV

The two tragedies in Ruth's background could have easily been reason for her to develop oily skin. First her husband died, followed by her brother-in-law. These circumstances could have dried her skin out. Tragedies have a way of shifting our lives either to the negative or the positive. Clearly Ruth's life was not a bed of roses.

⁶ When Naomi heard in Moab that the LORD had come to the aid of his people by providing food for them, she and her daughters-in-law prepared to return home from there. ⁷ With her two daughters-in-law she left the place where she had been living and set out on the road that would take them back to the land of Judah.⁸ Then Naomi said to her two daughters-in-law, "Go back, each of you, to your mother's home. May the LORD show you kindness, as you have shown kindness to your dead husbands and to me. ⁹ May the LORD grant that each of you will find rest in the home of another husband." Then she kissed them goodbye and they wept aloud ¹⁰ and said to her, "We will go back with you to your people."¹¹ But Naomi said, "Return home, my daughters. Why would you come with me? Am I going to have any more sons, who could become your husbands? ¹² Return home, my daughters; I am too old to have *another husband. Even if I thought there was still hope for me—even if I had a husband tonight and then gave birth to sons— ^{13} would you wait until they grew up? Would you remain unmarried for them? No, my daughters. It is more bitter for me than for you, because the LORD's hand has turned against me!"^{14} At this they wept aloud again. Then Orpah kissed her mother-in-law goodbye, but Ruth clung to her.*

--Ruth 1:6-14

In addition to Ruth's losses, she is now about to lose her mother-in-law. Ruth has a decision to make. Not only is Naomi leaving, she is emphatically discouraging Ruth and Orpah from coming along because she has nothing to offer them. Naomi is past childbearing years and could not have any more children. Even if she did, Ruth and Orpah would have to wait for them to mature before they could legally get married, and there was no guarantee Naomi would even have sons. Evidently Naomi was valuable to Ruth and Orpah for they took care of her and were dismayed by her leaving. Ultimately, Orpah decided to listen to Naomi's advice and left. But Ruth clung to Naomi.

When opportunity knocks, sometimes we don't hear it or we ignore it because it does not look like what we expected. Others see opportunity but turn and walk away. You must decide for yourself how to proceed when opportunity knocks. Apparently, there was something in Ruth that caused her to know that there was more to be expected than what she was able to see at that moment.

^{15} "Look," said Naomi, "your sister-in-law is going back to her people and her gods. Go back with her."^{16} But Ruth replied, "Don't urge me to leave you or to turn back from you. Where you go I will go, and where

you stay I will stay. Your people will be my people and your God my God. [17] *Where you die I will die, and there I will be buried. May the* LORD *deal with me, be it ever so severely, if even death separates you and me."* [18] *When Naomi realized that Ruth was determined to go with her, she stopped urging her.*

Even when Naomi tried to discourage Ruth, Ruth did not let go. She was determined, which is an attribute of normal skin. She didn't show fear, though she'd never been to Naomi's native land, she was willing to leave everything she knew. Ruth was willing to start a new life in a foreign place; willing to forsake all. She loved Naomi. She was selfless and more concerned about caring for Naomi than finding a comfortable life for herself. Ruth must have known her family was going to talk about her and people were not going to understand her decision, but she remained focused. She was humble in her vow to Naomi.

Ruth was determined and relentless in her pursuit of her vow. These are attributes we can carry over into every area of our lives. When it comes to our dreams, we must be fearless, determined and willing to sacrifice. We must be humble and not walk in pride. And many times we have to transition, make adjustments and step out into the unknown. This could be changing careers or pursuing a passion without a roadmap. This could be starting a ministry or a foundation. Whatever it may be, you need these attributes.

Now Naomi had a relative on her husband's side, a man of standing from the clan of Elimelek, whose name was Boaz. [2] *And Ruth the Moabite said to Naomi, "Let me go to the fields and pick up the leftover grain behind anyone in whose eyes I find favor." Naomi said to her, "Go ahead, my daughter."*

--Ruth 2:1-2 NIV

Ruth was willing to work. She said, "Let me go." She went not to have Naomi take care of her, but to take care of Naomi. Ruth had a plan. She was not going to just work in any field. She purposed what to look for, a place of favor. She was not sitting around waiting on a man. It was her work ethic, sacrifice, character and humility that caught Boaz's attention—not her eyes, lips or thighs. Many women are waiting around for life to come to them, but it is when we get in motion that things will begin to come together.

³ So she went out, entered a field and began to glean behind the harvesters. As it turned out, she was working in a field belonging to Boaz, who was from the clan of Elimelek.⁴ Just then Boaz arrived from Bethlehem and greeted the harvesters, "The LORD be with you!" "The LORD bless you!" they answered. ⁵ Boaz asked the overseer of his harvesters, "Who does that young woman belong to?" ⁶ The overseer replied, "She is the Moabite who came back from Moab with Naomi. ⁷ She said, 'Please let me glean and gather among the sheaves behind the harvesters.' She came into the field and has remained here from morning till now, except for a short rest in the shelter."

--Ruth 2:3-7 NIV

Ruth was respectful in her request to the servants. She also worked hard, which got the attention of Boaz. She was consistent; she didn't work for just one day and quit. She was timely, rising early in the morning to work. She was about business. These are all attributes of someone with normal skin.

⁸ So Boaz said to Ruth, "My daughter, listen to me. Don't go and glean in another field and don't go away from here. Stay here with the women who work for me. ⁹ Watch the field where the men are harvesting, and follow along after the women. I have told the men not to lay a hand on you. And whenever you are thirsty, go and get a drink from the water jars the men have filled."¹⁰ At this, she bowed down with her face to the ground. She asked him, "Why have I found such favor in your eyes that you notice me—a foreigner?"¹¹ Boaz replied, "I've been told all about what you have done for your mother-in-law since the death of your husband—how you left your father and mother and your homeland and came to live with a people you did not know before. ¹² May the LORD repay you for what you have done. May you be richly rewarded by the LORD, the God of Israel, under whose wings you have come to take refuge."

-- Ruth 2:8-12 NIV

Ruth did not have to chase Boaz; her credibility spoke for her. At that point, Boaz took control of the situation. There is no mention of Ruth's physical appearance at all. What appealed to Boaz was Ruth's dedication and noble character. She had pure motives and her purity spoke through her work ethic. What does your work ethic say? What does it fully reveal about you? Is it negative or positive?

Through her faithfulness, Ruth found favor, shelter and a covering. Boaz married Ruth and their marriage brought restoration to Naomi. When you take care of God's business through obedience and humility, He will keep you covered and bless you. Ruth is an example of someone who persevered through situations that could have caused her to have oily, dry, combination or sensitive spiritual skin. Yet she maintained her normal skin. She did not allow situations to determine her virtues, attributes or the quality of her love. She stayed pure in heart, humble in speech, and obedient in her actions. Ruth epitomizes someone with normal skin.

I have been blessed to watch friends wait on the Lord. What they received was more than worth the wait. They, like Ruth, were hardworking, submissive and diligent. They allowed themselves to be processed, cleansed and healed. They walked in character and integrity. Their beauty is more than skin deep. They have substance, depth and value. When they met their prospective mates, they were not looking for a man to take care of them. They each brought something to the table. Is it fair for us as women to want so much from men, yet not offer the same in return?

We do not necessarily need to bring a huge bank account to the relationship; however, there are some things that we should have in order. If you have credit challenges, begin working on them. Take responsibility for your life, the good and the bad. Address and deal with your emotional status and get healed. Address your physical status by maintaining a healthy lifestyle. Do not wait until Boaz comes, start working right now!

Ruth did not allow where she came from to determine her destiny. She was willing to take a risk to better her life while caring for someone else. She was not selfish, she was giving; she was not lazy, she was hard working. Ruth was not passive, she was determined; she was not weak, she was strong. Ruth was not a prideful woman, she was humble. Ruth could have followed Orpah, but she made a decision that blessed her in ways she could have never imagined. What does God have for you in His plan and His purpose? What is in your field? What will you reap? What will be your reward? Time will tell; however, you must be willing to surrender all, be humble and teachable, hardworking and diligent.

Are you waiting? Are you looking? Are you working? Are you watching? For those who are not in the field, the time is now. For those working in the field, keep trusting God. Make sure you keep your heart clean and your motives pure. There is a quote by the late poet Maya Angelou which says, "A woman's heart should be so lost in God that a man must seek Him in order to find her." Let that be you. Know that you are worth the wait.

Prayer

Father please help me to understand my value and that I'm worth the wait. Let me no longer compromise myself for a moment of pleasure or satisfaction. Let me get to work in the areas I know need maintenance. Connect me with women of wisdom who will give Godly instruction and advice. Revive my dreams and passions and show me the path to pursue them. Let new determination, humility and strong work ethics be found in me in this season of my life.

Chapter 10
The Ripple Effect

"There's a ripple effect in all we do –What you do, touches me; What I do, touches you." (Author unknown)

From the time you were conceived until this very moment, you have been creating ripples, knowingly and unknowingly. Even when you are no longer here, your ripple will continue. Webster's defines a ripple effect as a gradually spreading effect or influence: the repercussions of an event or situation experienced far beyond its immediate location, or a spreading effect or series of consequences caused by a single action or event. Your ripple effect touches friends, family, co-workers, neighbors and complete strangers.

Everyone reading this book is a living, breathing ripple effect. We each have a choice about the type of ripples we want to be. By our words, attitudes and actions, we release more ripples and waves than we can imagine. Have you ever been in not the best mood and a stranger smiles at you? Most of the time you cannot help but to smile back. In that moment, another person's attitude ripple-affected you. Now think of how many of these kinds of instances occur daily, and think of what types of ripples you are releasing through your words and actions.

The most powerful tool in determining our ripple is our tongue. The words we speak can cause either calm or explosive ripples. They can foster peace or create destruction. We have the ability to speak life or death over situations. Therefore, we must consciously speak words that we want to see materialize. Unfortunately, oftentimes people speak before they think, and when words are released, we are unable to take them back.

I saw this quote and thought it was very powerful and had to share: "Words and hearts should be handled with care for words when spoken and hearts when broken are the hardest thing to repair." Take a moment and think about the unique way that words affect you. Nothing else really causes deep hurt and trauma in the way that words do. Words spoken or written have the power to shift attitudes, atmospheres and change lives. Nothing really discourages or motivates like words do. Words truly have power. Words literally are the framework of who we are and who we can become.

What ripple effect does your behavior create? Your behavior affects not only you, but everything you touch. Our behavior is often an external reflection of what is going on internally. When we feel good inside, we generally reflect that by smiling or laughing. When we are frustrated or angry, we can reflect that by rolling our eyes or being sharp and short with people. Whatever behavior we reflect, it has an effect on us and those around us. This quote was a most interesting find while doing some research: "A bad attitude is like a flat tire. If you don't change it, you won't go anywhere." Is your attitude causing you to be stuck in situations?

Sarah was the wife of the Abraham, who is known as the father of faith. Sarah certainly played a huge role in the 'Abraham story' since she was his wife; that makes her the mother of faith. Through reading the word, we are able to see how her combination skin caused ripples, which still impact us today. Sarah was certainly a woman of valor; however, she still had some oiliness and breakouts. Let's look further into the ripples she released.

The LORD had said to Abram, "Go from your country, your people and your father's household to the land I will show you.[2] "I will make you into a great nation, and I will bless you; I will make your name great, and you will be a blessing[3] I will bless those who bless you, and whoever curses you I will curse; and all peoples on earth will be blessed through you.[4] So Abram went, as the LORD had told him; and Lot went with him. Abram was seventy-five years old when he set out from Harran.[5] He took his wife Sarai, his nephew Lot, all the possessions they had accumulated and the people they had acquired in Harran, and they set out for the land of Canaan, and they arrived there.

-- Genesis 12:1-5

Not only did Abraham leave his family, country and everything he knew, but Sarah did as well. They were both dedicated and courageous in believing and following the word of God, in order to receive the promise of God. This promise was loaded with blessings that were beyond their human comprehension. The promise showed the favor of God for them, the protection of God over them and the purpose of God in them. However, the only way to walk into this promise was through obedience. Sarah was willing to leave the familiar, family and comfort, to be led by God and her husband. This is a reflection of the normal parts of Sarah's skin. Obedience and submission are two necessary traits for someone with normal spiritual skin.

I also want to point out Sarah was not a young woman when she took this journey. If Abraham was 75, she wasn't too many years behind.

Her age alone shows the courage of this woman. Many would say that it is easier to leave all when you are young, but what about when you're older? So many relationships established, a comfortable and stable life deeply rooted in your community. She chose to forsake all of this and was willing to uproot herself for the sake of obedience. Sarah's story teaches us that you are never too old to pursue the promises of God. Ask yourself how would you and your family respond if your 70-year-old grandmother told the family she was leaving to go to place she has no knowledge of to obtain a promise from the Lord? What type of ripple effect would that create amongst your family and friends?

Beauty is a topic that is constantly discussed through media, movies, magazines, and most other aspects of our daily lives. There is a constant quest for the perfect beauty products or to create the "perfect" look. Many wish for and desire changes so they can "be" beautiful. As much as we talk about it, many never consider the other side of what beauty can bring. Sarah is one of the few people in the bible who is described physically. Her name alone means "princess." On more than one occasion, we are told that she was beautiful or fair to look upon. Most would say her beauty was a positive in her life. However, while beauty can be a blessing, it also brings challenges.

[12] When the Egyptians see you, they will say, 'This is his wife.' Then they will kill me but will let you live. [13] Say you are my sister, so that I will be treated well for your sake and my life will be spared because of you. [14] When Abram came to Egypt, the Egyptians saw that Sarai was a very beautiful woman. [15] And when Pharaoh's officials saw her, they praised her to Pharaoh, and she was taken into his palace. [16] He treated Abram well for her sake, and Abram acquired sheep and cattle, male and

female donkeys, male and female servants, and camels.^{17} *But the* LORD *inflicted serious diseases on Pharaoh and his household because of Abram's wife Sarai.*

-- Genesis 12:12-17

Sarah's beauty caused Abraham to devise a plan to protect his life through deceit. In going along with the plan, Sarah was taken into the Pharaoh's house. Ultimately, Abraham and Sarah's lie caused a ripple effect of great plagues in Pharaoh's home. The Lord honored his promise and, in spite of their deceit, He protected and rescued them. How many of you ever thought a lie based on physical beauty could have this type of effect? In the next verses, we learn that when Pharaoh discovered that Sarah was really the wife of Abraham, he released them both. Sadly, the lesson was not learned and this was not the only instance of this type of deceit. Ten years later - the same story, just a different king.

And Abraham journeyed from thence toward the south country, and dwelled between Kadesh and Shur, and sojourned in Gerar.^{2} *And Abraham said of Sarah his wife, She is my sister: and Abimelech king of Gerar sent, and took Sarah.*^{3} *But God came to Abimelech in a dream by night, and said to him, Behold, thou art but a dead man, for the woman which thou hast taken; for she is a man's wife.*^{4} *But Abimelech had not come near her: and he said, LORD, wilt thou slay also a righteous nation?*^{5} *Said he not unto me, She is my sister? and she, even she herself said, He is my brother: in the integrity of my heart and innocency of my hands have I done this.*^{6} *And God said unto him in a dream, Yea, I know that thou didst this in the integrity of thy heart; for I also withheld thee*

95

from sinning against me: therefore suffered I thee not to touch her. [7] *Now therefore restore the man his wife; for he is a prophet, and he shall pray for thee, and thou shalt live: and if thou restore her not, know thou that thou shalt surely die, thou, and all that are thine.* [8] *Therefore Abimelech rose early in the morning, and called all his servants, and told all these things in their ears: and the men were sore afraid.* [9] *Then Abimelech called Abraham, and said unto him, What hast thou done unto us? and what have I offended thee, that thou hast brought on me and on my kingdom a great sin? thou hast done deeds unto me that ought not to be done.* [10] *And Abimelech said unto Abraham, What sawest thou, that thou hast done this thing?* [11] *And Abraham said, Because I thought, Surely the fear of God is not in this place; and they will slay me for my wife's sake.*

-- Genesis 20:1-11

What type of beauty did this woman possess for the same lie to be required ten years later? I believe Sarah's physical beauty was a reflection of an inner beauty radiating outwardly. Sarah's beauty caused her husband to fear for his life and their lies to protect him still placed them in dangerous situations. The ripple effect of their deceit brought distress, plagues and barrenness to innocent people. The servants and maidservants of both the Pharaoh and Abimelech had nothing to do with the situation, yet they were affected negatively from Sarah and Abraham's decision. Beauty comes with a price, and a responsibility. The ripples caused by refusing to deal with the responsibility directly can be destructive on a great scale.

Although Sarah was certainly courageous and was given beauty and a precious promise, her life still had challenges.

Now Sarai was childless because she was not able to conceive.

--Genesis 11:30

Sarah was a beautiful woman married to a man with means, but she was missing something, a child. During that time a woman's value was measured by her fertility, and Sarah had been barren for decades. Can you imagine how that made her feel? She was a noblewoman, the wife of a strong leader, yet unable to produce an heir for him. The shame must have been unbearable.

Now Sarai, Abram's wife, had borne him no children. But she had an Egyptian slave named Hagar; ² so she said to Abram, "The LORD has kept me from having children. Go, sleep with my slave; perhaps I can build a family through her." Abram agreed to what Sarai said. ³ So after Abram had been living in Canaan ten years, Sarai his wife took her Egyptian slave Hagar and gave her to her husband to be his wife. ⁴ He slept with Hagar, and she conceived. When she knew she was pregnant, she began to despise her mistress.

-- Genesis 16:1-4

In light of the previous stories we shouldn't really be shocked that both Abraham and Sarah were schemers. Sarah knew that she had been given a promise, but due to "body clocks" ticking she decided to "help" God. Her plan did produce a child, but the birth did not come peacefully. Although Abraham and Hagar were successful, in creating a child, their union caused much strife and discord. Hagar's "success" caused her to be despised. She actually ran away for a while but returned out of obedience to God.

Have you ever received a word or promise that seems impossible? Even if you have hope initially, as time passes, that hope can begin to fade away and you may feel the need to 'help' the promise come to pass. It had been years since Abraham and Sarah stepped out on faith, in obedience to God, and Sarah still had not produced a child. She suggested Hagar as a surrogate to her husband to ensure that an heir was produced, even if not by her. I believe this was one of the hardest decisions of Sarah's life. Each year when a birthday would come, she watched the chance of reproducing dwindle away before her very eyes.

Hagar produced not only a child but a son, which was needed to carry on the family name and legacy. The successful birth of Ishmael, the heir produced as a result of Sarah's plan, caused her to despise the very method that she suggested. Isn't that something? We devise a plan and then get angry when it comes out exactly the way we devised it. I believe Sarah's reaction was rooted more in hurt, anger and disappointment in herself; however, she released these emotions on Hagar. What may have seemed to be a reasonable strategy was not the plan of God. Sarah's plan set in motion a ripple effect that she could never reverse.

This teaches us that when we try to "help" God, we may get something, but it will not come with His peace. His timetable is perfect; we just have to wait. Some would think that since Sarah tried to "help" God, He would not keep His word to her. That she had broken His promise. But that was not the case. God was forgiving and faithful to Sarah and Abraham and kept His promise to them.

[15] God also said to Abraham, "As for Sarai your wife, you are no longer to call her Sarai; her name will be Sarah. [16] I will bless her and will surely give you a son by her. I will bless her so that she will be the mother of nations; kings of peoples will come from her."

--Genesis 17:15-16

Let me remind you that this new promise was given *after* Sarah had schemed and lied. I'm not condoning her actions; however, this shows how God looks beyond us and our mistakes and still desires to fulfill the purpose He has for us. It is rare that you see a name changed in the bible. This is symbolic of covenant. Her name went from "princess" to "noble lady." She who was once childless would not only birth her own child at the age of 90, but she would also be the mother of many.

Sarah's ripple effect of courage, loyalty and faithfulness is still having an impact on us today. Although at moments she doubted and had fear, she is one of the few mentioned in the hall of faith found in Hebrews 11.

And by faith even Sarah, who was past childbearing age, was enabled to bear children because she considered him faithful who had made the promise.

--Hebrews 11:11

There is much we can learn from Sarah. Her journey was filled with many twists and turns. Her combination skin was rooted in the positive and negative intentions of her actions and decisions. She had so much influence with her words, attitude and actions that she affected people both positively and negatively. Sarah was used mightily by God even in her frailties and moments of fear. Because, even in those moments, Sarah never lost faith in God's promise, though she may have lost faith in His method. In spite of her insufficiencies, she is truly a beautiful example and we can gain so much from her.

Have you been feeling a wooing and a beckoning to go on a journey with God? What was the promise to you? Have you taken the first step? If not, what is stopping you? Are you to go alone or with someone else? If you were asked to leave the familiar, family and comfort, would you? If not, why not? What would hinder you? What kind of ripples and waves are you setting into motion by your words, attitude, and actions?

You may not see the shore on which each rippling wave lands, but the shore where you stand right now is where the ripple must begin. Make your ripples purposeful!!!

Prayer

Father, by an act of my will, I choose to make my words, actions and attitude a positive ripple effect. I ask that You set a guard around my mouth that I may speak that which is pleasing to You. Bridle my tongue and let wisdom rule even if that means being silent. From this day forward, I will bless and not curse. I will build up and not tear down. I will plant and not tear apart. I will encourage and not discourage. Forgive me for when I've used my tongue, attitude and actions for evil and not good. Cause me to be ever the more sensitive to the influence and impact I have in the lives of others. Let me be one who leaves great, lasting deposits that will bring You glory. Like Sarah, give me the strength to conceive the seed, the purpose and the dream You have given

100

me. Let me be found faithful. I choose to make my ripples powerful and purposeful. I pray for wisdom with my words. I will make the necessary adjustments to stay in alignment with You.

Chapter 11
Tows & Tickets

Decisions

In order to transition to the new you must reconcile the old, this will require you to be honest and bold.

In order to receive the unseen you must first believe, you can't be confused, unfocused or deceived.

In order to move forward you can't still be looking back, in doing so you won't get on the right track.

In order to have a heart healed you must first release, this may not be easy but will bring you so much peace.

In order to build you must first count the cost, examining former battles won and loss.

In order to receive you must have an open hand, giving to others whenever you can.

In order to have wisdom you can simply ask, but also be willing to follow instructions and complete task.

In order to receive honor you must be humble, pride will hinder you and cause you to stumble.

In order to prepare for increase you must be pruned, allow the adjustments and be fine-tuned.

In order to love you must be real, dishonesty and lack of integrity will destroy any seal.

In order to progress you must get rid of the weights, too much baggage will keep you out of doors and gates.

In order to transition decisions must be made, you must be stable and constant not easily swayed.

In order to see that which only you've seen in dreams come true, make decisions based from Gods point of view.

We live in such a fast paced society that many of us are just moving through life without taking the time to pause. Our society's intense speed can cause us to become exhausted and overwhelmed. Finding balance is necessary so that we don't spin out of control. You cannot drive a car continually without getting maintenance. The car will malfunction and place you and everyone around you in danger.

I remember driving on the expressway and the brake light came on in my car. The brake light had come on before, so I thought I just needed to add brake fluid. On my way to work, I stopped by an auto store and picked some up. I put it in the car and thought I would be fine. To my dismay, when I proceeded to drive home, the brake light came on again, but this time it was blinking. I became uncomfortable and actually a bit frightened. I checked the car manual, which stated that if this happened, I needed to see a mechanic immediately. Since my job required a lot of highway driving, the fear increased as to what could happen if I didn't get this fixed immediately. I was blessed to have a co-worker who knew a mechanic only two miles away, and he was able to service my vehicle that same day. Although my pockets were lighter because of the expense, I had peace of mind when I drove home that day.

We cannot keep going nonstop without emotional and spiritual balance checks and tune ups. We can hurt ourselves and those around us if we don't. Once we have balanced out, it will be easier to gauge when we are getting off-kilter. The process may take only a day, but it could also take a weekend or month—take as long as you need to achieve complete balance.

Some relationships are like parking meters. As we've been on the road of life, some of us have been looking for new places to park, or find valid, quality relationships were we can rest a while. We may have been searching for minutes, hours, days, even years. And when we finally find an available space that we really want, we try to hold on to it. However, the length of time we can park is determined by how much time is on the parking meter. The meter's location may also be an important factor in determining the amount of time allotted.

Relationships can be likened to parking spots in a metropolitan district. The amount of time allotted for each relationship will vary from individual to individual based on a variety of factors. Some people will come into our lives for a short time, like 20 minute parking spaces in busy areas, and then their time in our lives will expire. When our emotions are settled, like a large paved parking lot, people may come into our lives and stay for longer periods of time. The point is that there is a timeframe for every relationship. Some are meant to last a lifetime, but many have time limits. Many of us ignore these limits and end up with tickets.

After you find that coveted parking space, you have to pay the meter. We have to make sure we have enough resources to put into the meter so that we do not get a ticket. When our paid time is up and the "expired" light flashes, we will be given a ticket if we don't move. The key is to monitor our time and make it back before the meter expires. Unfortunately, some of us get caught up and do not get back in time. This is the equivalent of getting caught up in a relationship that was only designed to last a short time. When we over-extended the relationship, we end up having to pay a high emotional ticket. The fee for an emotional ticket is the unnecessary drama and emotional baggage that occur at the end of an over-stayed relationship.

Lot's wife is an example of someone with dry skin who received overstayed her meter and received an expensive emotional ticket. The Bible does not provide dialogue; however, we can glean information about her from the scriptures and use the lesson of her life to better ourselves. Being married to Abraham's nephew connected Lot's wife to wealth. It also connected her to favor. For God honored Lot and decided, before destroying the land, that He would send help to Lot and his family.

It is not clear how long Lot lived in Sodom, but we can assume it was for a good amount of years. During that time, Lot and his wife would have had to tolerate the sins of that city. We don't know if Lot's wife engaged in any of the sin or if she hated it; however, all we know is that she stayed with Lot in that vile place known for strong sexual perversion, immorality, idolatry and drunkenness.

When Lot's wife is first mentioned, a lot that has already taken place in the course of the narrative. God has already decided to destroy the cities of Sodom and Gomorrah, but He sends angels to rescue Lot and his family first.

The two angels arrived at Sodom in the evening, and Lot was sitting in the gateway of the city. When he saw them, he got up to meet them and bowed down with his face to the ground. [2] *"My lords," he said, "please turn aside to your servant's house. You can wash your feet and spend the night and then go on your way early in the morning." "No," they answered, "we will spend the night in the square."* [3] *But he insisted so*

strongly that they did go with him and entered his house. He prepared a
meal for them, baking bread without yeast, and they ate.

-- *Genesis 19:1-3*

Lot's wife probably did the cooking and the cleaning for these angels. She listened to the conversation at dinner and knew that God had sent help. She didn't have much time left in her parking spot. She would have to leave everything she had grown to love because her meter was about to expire.

[15] *With the coming of dawn, the angels urged Lot, saying, "Hurry! Take your wife and your two daughters who are here, or you will be swept away when the city is punished."* [16] *When he hesitated, the men grasped his hand and the hands of his wife and of his two daughters and led them safely out of the city, for the* LORD *was merciful to them.* [17] *As soon as they had brought them out, one of them said, "Flee for your lives! Don't look back, and don't stop anywhere in the plain! Flee to the mountains or you will be swept away!"*

-- *Genesis 19:15-17*

Lot and his family were given specific instructions to follow. It was made plain to them what to do and what not to do. In the Word of God there are instructions, which we are to follow with precision. This requires us to take responsibility for our actions. Every day God is trying to make a way of escape for us. He's trying to prevent us from getting a ticket. The question is, will we follow His instructions?

24 Then the LORD rained down burning sulfur on Sodom and Gomorrah—from the LORD out of the heavens. 25 Thus he overthrew those cities and the entire plain, destroying all those living in the cities—and also the vegetation in the land. 26 But Lot's wife looked back, and she became a pillar of salt.

--Genesis 19:24-26

Unfortunately, Lot's wife was enveloped in and betrayed by the sensitivity of her dry skin. Although she entertained angels and was aware of the urgency of the situation and the seriousness of their instructions, somewhere in her heart, she could not let go. Lot's wife tried to hold on to the past instead of moving into her future. She overstayed her relationship with Sodom and got a ticket, one that cost her life. But her punishment was not hers alone to bear. Just like the unintended financial consequence a parking ticket can have on a family, the emotional ticket Lot's wife paid detrimentally affected the lives of everyone she left behind.

The decisions we make impact other people. Our lives affect our family, friends, acquaintances and even strangers. When we are disobedient and do not follow instructions others will be affected, sometimes severely. When the way of escape is revealed, will you obey God? Or will you allow your desire for the world you are leaving behind to cause you to look back?

A trick of the enemy is to distract and cause you to lose focus. We have to keep track of the time and make sure that we don't overstay situations in our lives. If we listen, the Holy Spirit will let us know when we are coming close to the "expired" light. The Holy Spirit will let us know when a relationship is coming to an end or when a fellowship is over. However, we must make the decision to either listen to that word and separate expeditiously or stay longer than allotted and face the consequences. A parking ticket can be very costly and it accrues additional fees over time if not paid in full right away. Likewise, the cost of staying in a relationship that has expired can amount to an exorbitant mental, emotional and physical penalty.

Many times the signs of a relationship expiring can be sensed with our natural abilities. The conversation changes and feels awkward. The comfort level also changes. You may find yourself arguing or yelling or just plain aggravated after being in the person's company. And, just like you have to get into your car and move on to the next location, you must decide to move on from the relationship. When the light starts blinking, make sure you do not overstay. The meter man is waiting.

Prayer

Father, help me to be honest about the state of my life and the people I've embraced. Show me those who I've held on to longer than I should and why I've not let them go. Give me wisdom to handle each relationship in a way that is pleasing to You. Forgive me for any anger or bitterness I may harbor from the effects of being in a relationship longer than the time allotted. Cause me to be led by You and to also obey the instructions given. Let me no longer extend relationships that have expired. I will embrace the new that You have for me.

Chapter 12

What's Your Beauty Score?

When we get ready to make large purchases like a car or a house, or to apply for a loan, our credit score is usually the determining factor as to whether we are approved or denied. Our score is affected by how we handle our finances. Do you pay your bills on time? How many open lines of credit do you have? How many major credit cards do you have? Do you have store credit cards? Are you current on your student loans? Have you filed for bankruptcy? These are just a few factors that affect our credit rating. If our credit score is low, we can change it, but it is going to take work. It takes discipline, a budget and clear goals. Some may wonder, "What does a credit score have to do with beauty or holiness?" I'm glad you asked.

When discussing external beauty people generally rate or measure it on a scale of 1-10. I would like to use that analogy for spiritual beauty, but instead of using a 10-point scale, I would like to parallel a natural credit score with a spiritual score. Our spiritual score isn't based on finances. It is determined by the level of our reflection of Christ. When we reflect Him, the beauty of His holiness shines through us. What we do, what we say and how we respond to situations are indicators of how much we mirror Christ's image just like the factors above are indicators of our credit score. So when we look to determine our spiritual score, we should focus on how much we display the fruit of the Spirit.

[4] *Remain in me, as I also remain in you. No branch can bear fruit by itself; it must remain in the vine. Neither can you bear fruit unless you*

remain in me.[5] *"I am the vine; you are the branches. If you remain in me and I in you, you will bear much fruit; apart from me you can do nothing.*

-- *John 15:4-5*

The fruit borne in and through our lives are indicators of how connected we are to the Vine, which is Christ. The closer our connection, the more fruit we bear. The farther away we are, the fewer fruit we bear.

How much love, joy, peace, longsuffering, gentleness, goodness, faith and meekness do you exhibit? The fruit of the spirit are the reflection of Christ in you and indicators of your spiritual score. Do you pray, praise, fast, worship or study? Just like credit repair services, these actions help to keep us connected to the Vine, thereby increasing our fruit yield and spiritual credit score.

Most people don't actively check their credit scores on a daily basis. Some people check their credit report once a month, some once every six months, some once a year. We can actually register with websites that will give us our score on a monthly basis so that we are regularly informed of its status. Since we have the right to dispute information on our report, it is helpful to keep up to date on its status. Spiritually, the Holy Spirit makes us aware of our spiritual credit score. He will inform us when we handle situations in ways that can cause our score to move in a positive or negative direction. Just as financial discipline is the key to a natural credit score, obedience is the key to our spiritual credit score. The more obedient we are, the closer we will be to Christ, increasing our spiritual score.

Spiritually, we can dispute our credit report through repentance. When we receive salvation, our slate is washed clean and our score is elevated. However, based on how we live and walk out our salvation our score may go up or down from time to time. When we harbor bitterness, jealousy, unforgiveness, anger, pride, covetousness, it sends our spiritual score plummeting. Repentance deletes the negative items from our spiritual credit score. Spiritual credit is not based on how many years we have been in the church or have claimed salvation. It is based on the evidence of the fruit of the Spirit operating in our life, the reflection of our heart and our willingness to mature in Christ. Our score increases the more we fast and pray and study God's Word. It rises as we willingly apply the truths of the Word to our daily lives. This score is not something we can keep count of alone or in an app; its record is found in heaven and Jesus is the accountant.

Mary Magdalene is a great example of how to change both oily skin and your spiritual credit score. Mary is known in the scriptures as the woman from whom Jesus cast out seven demons. She had really bad credit. We do not know how or when she became bound with the spirits, or if all seven spirits came at one time. What we do know is that, when she encountered Jesus, all seven spirits had her bound. Anytime we are bound, there is an element of torment. Can you imagine walking around with seven negative spirits inside of you? The sheer number of unclean spirits is evidence that sin was active in her life. Her spiritual skin was the definition of oily and difficult to treat. She was not battling one thing but seven. She was not dealing with one issue but seven. She did not have one struggle to overcome, but seven.

And certain woman, which had been healed of evil spirits and infirmities,

Mary called Magdalene, out of whom went seven devils.

Unclean spirits not only bind you spiritually, they can also bring physical, emotional, psychological and even financial ills. Oily skin affects every area of our life. Although we may continue to function in society, we will have limitations. A negative credit score limits you in society. What you can buy, where you can live, even what job you can have. That is why we dispute credit reports and attempt to rehabilitate our credit, to give us a clean slate. When we meet Mary, she is healed. Jesus healed Mary and cleared her credit report. He can and will do the same for us.

In the bulk of the scriptures, Mary Magdalene is with Mary, the mother of Jesus. Once Mary Magdalene was healed and delivered, she connected herself to a woman of power. That says a lot. From what I gather, she probably no longer associated with anyone or anything that reminded her of the seven spirits she was delivered from. She connected with people who had good credit scores. Her whole life changed and so did her focus. Once she was set free from her oily skin, she made every effort to keep it clean and healthy. She was so grateful for her deliverance that she stayed close to the One who had set her free. This is a good example to follow. When Jesus sets us free, we must stay close to Him. It is only through His word, prayer and repentance, fasting and worship, that we will be able to keep our skin normal.

[37] A woman in that town who lived a sinful life learned that Jesus was eating at the Pharisee's house, so she came there with an alabaster jar of perfume. [38] As she stood behind him at his feet weeping, she began to wet

112

his feet with her tears. Then she wiped them with her hair, kissed them and poured perfume on them.[39] *When the Pharisee who had invited him saw this, he said to himself, "If this man were a prophet, he would know who is touching him and what kind of woman she is—that she is a sinner."*

--Luke 7:37-39

Although the scripture does not provide a name, many scholars and theologians believe that it was Mary Magdalene who anointed the feet of Jesus. When she approached Jesus, she was not given an invitation, and she knew that she would not be welcomed, but she didn't stop—she was focused. Look at the description above. They called her a sinner. She was not just a sinner by her own description, she was known in the city as a sinner. People had access to her credit report. The sins she committed were not hidden. Her sinful lifestyle was well known in the community. But that did not stop Mary Magdalene. Too many of us get caught up in our surroundings and the worries of people knowing our history but, like Mary Magdalene, we must remain focused on Jesus.

Mary Magdalene was so thankful and grateful for what Jesus had done for her that she put herself into an uncomfortable position in order to have the chance to bless Him. The community may not have gotten it but Mary Magdalene had the updated credit report. She had been healed and set free, and she did not need to explain this to anyone or get the community's confirmation. She knew what people were thinking and saying, yet she kept moving towards Jesus. Likewise, we must keep moving closer to Jesus. And we must be willing to sacrifice to get to Him. The oil Mary Magdalene purchased was very costly, she did not buy Him something cheap. The oil was very valuable, and she was willing to use it on Jesus' feet. Mary Magdalene understood she could not repay Him; however, she humbled herself and gave Him the best that she had. Mary Magdalene's oily skin had become normal.

[40] Jesus answered him, "Simon, I have something to tell you." "Tell me, teacher," he said.[41] "Two people owed money to a certain moneylender. One owed him five hundred denarii and the other fifty. [42] Neither of them had the money to pay him back, so he forgave the debts of both. Now which of them will love him more?"[43] Simon replied, "I suppose the one who had the bigger debt forgiven." "You have judged correctly," Jesus said. [44] Then he turned toward the woman and said to Simon, "Do you see this woman? I came into your house. You did not give me any water for my feet, but she wet my feet with her tears and wiped them with her hair. [45] You did not give me a kiss, but this woman, from the time I entered, has not stopped kissing my feet. [46] You did not put oil on my head, but she has poured perfume on my feet. [47] Therefore, I tell you, her many sins have been forgiven—as her great love has shown. But whoever has been forgiven little loves little." [48] Then Jesus said to her, "Your sins are forgiven."

--Luke 7:40-48

In this passage we see the compassion of Christ. He knew who the woman was and He knew all of her sins. She knew how to worship and show appreciation for her deliverance. She understood the value of what He did in her life while those watching did not. Because she was so grateful, there was no need for her to defend her actions; Jesus spoke on her account.

³ While he was in Bethany, reclining at the table in the home of Simon the Leper, a woman came with an alabaster jar of very expensive perfume, made of pure nard. She broke the jar and poured the perfume on his head.⁴ Some of those present were saying indignantly to one another, "Why this waste of perfume? ⁵ It could have been sold for more than a year's wages and the money given to the poor." And they rebuked her harshly.⁶ "Leave her alone," said Jesus. "Why are you bothering her? She has done a beautiful thing to me.

--Mark 14:3-6

Once again, the woman did not have to defend or explain herself. She came to Jesus as she was, holding nothing back. She was humbled before Him and gave Him her best. In doing so, Jesus showed her favor, corrected the crowd, and then He blessed her, forgave her and made her a testimony. Like Mary Magdalene, we have to press past adversity and keep doing the will of God while others are talking. He alone can forgive, bless and establish us.

¹Six days before the Passover, Jesus came to Bethany, where Lazarus lived, whom Jesus had raised from the dead. ² Here a dinner was given in Jesus' honor. Martha served, while Lazarus was among those reclining at the table with him. ³ Then Mary took about a pint of pure nard, an expensive perfume; she poured it on Jesus' feet and wiped his feet with her hair. And the house was filled with the fragrance of the perfume.

-- John 12:3

115

When you praise God with full abandonment of heart, it changes the atmosphere. Just like the fragrance filled the whole house, praise will filter into every part of who you are. It will not only filter, it will overpower everything it comes into contact with. Your problems will seem smaller. Mountains won't seem as large. Obstacles won't seem as big when you worship. Mary Magdalene was in the place where Jesus beckons many of us, a place of full complete surrender and focus on Him.

⁹ Truly I tell you, wherever the gospel is preached throughout the world, what she has done will also be told, in memory of her."

-- Mark 14:9

We must remember this was a woman with oily skin, who was known in the city as a sinner. She was a woman who was bound with seven demons. Although Jesus knows our past, He focuses on our future. He sees our hurt and has our healing in His hands. Jesus delivered Mary Magdalene and she became a woman of courage and honor. She was willing to walk into a place of controversy to anoint Jesus. Jesus set Mary Magdalene free because he saw through who she was to who she could be. And He is willing to do the same for each of us.

What is your credit score? Do you have some negative accounts that can be turned positive by forgiving people? Do you have some positive scores that you can increase by showing more love? Do you have some old relationships that you need to release because they have become negative accounts? Have you been reading the Word and increasing your devotional time to increase your reflection of Him? There are so many factors that can affect your score. Based on what you

116

know of yourself right now, what is your true spiritual credit score? If you don't know, ask Jesus—He's been monitoring your account.

Prayer

Father, show me my spiritual credit report. Although I may have an idea, I would like to see the account You've been keeping concerning me. I repent for the negative marks, and I yield myself to You. I will not walk in disobedience or rebellion in my thoughts and actions. I vow to be a worshipper. I thank you for saving, redeeming and cleansing me. I repent for allowing the cares of this world to blur and shadow the significance of the cross and repentance. Let a fresh understanding of your love and grace be released to me. Cause me to have single focus with full clarity.

Chapter 13

Truth & Deception

We can want something so badly that we will ignore the truth. Fasting and prayer can reveal the truth. The question is, will we receive the truth or turn away from it?

At a former job I met a nice looking young man. There was an immediate attraction and we exchanged numbers. He started attending my church and was baptized. As a person who is a giver, I did a lot for him. Apparently, I was doing so much for him that one day my dad told me to slow down. Although everyone in the family liked him, my dad said, as a man, there were things he observed that were not positive. So I slowed down, and that is when I began to notice some significant areas were deficient in my friend's character. Firstly, not only was he not a giver, he was actually very selfish. We had many disagreements where he just did not seem to understand the concept of giving, yet he fully understood receiving. Secondly, and more disturbing, I realized that I was not a priority to him.

I am a former tri-athlete. I played volleyball, basketball and ran track, so I understand sports. I actually love to watch football but rarely watch basketball. However, he liked a particular NBA team, which I couldn't stand. He knew this, yet on Valentine's Day, he bought me some half dead flowers and wanted to watch his team play. The red light was blaring: DANGER-DANGER-DANGER-SELFISH-SELFISH-SELFISH. After this event and many internal conversations, I told him, "You know, I need to find out why you came into my life. Was it for me to re-introduce you to God? Was it for us? Why are you actually here?" I told him I needed a week off and that I had to fast and pray about it. After my experiences, I have come to suggest this as a first step in considering a new relationship, instead of waiting until after emotional attachments have already started to form. During that week off, I found out people were encouraging him to send me flowers or some other visible gesture that he wanted stay in a relationship with me. He sent nothing.

When our "week off" concluded, he picked me up to take me out on a date. We had a good conversation in the car as we headed to Ft. Lauderdale's beach area. In my mind, I knew he had something planned. He pulled into the parking lot of Barnes and Noble and I thought, *Okay, he knows I like books. Not sure about this, but we'll see.* We went inside and looked at books and CDs, but purchased nothing. To my surprise, after only thirty-minutes, we were headed back to the car. I thought we would continue toward the beach for dinner and then a nice walk, but instead he drove us back in the direction we came from. I asked him where we were going. His reply: "Home. That was the date." I felt my temperature rise. I said, "So after a week of me trying to decide if this is going to work, your concept of a date is to look at books?"

I was completely astonished by his reply: "I didn't want to waste my money." To put it mildly, in ten seconds, I went from 0 to 1,000 in that car. I was more than heated. In my mind I kept hearing: *I know I was not just associated with the word "waste."* I informed him he didn't ever have to worry about 'wasting' money on me and to take me home.

That word *waste* was like a dagger to my heart. I know I'm valuable and precious, and he considered spending money, time and energy on me a waste? Of course he tried to explain that's not what he meant, but those words came from his heart. At that moment, I had to decide whether to shrug this off because he was considered a good guy, smart, funny, and people thought we should be together—or to go with my heart, knowing that I'm worth more and there is someone who won't ever see or speak of me in those terms. Needless to say, the relationship was over and, although he still came to church and tried to talk about it, I was done.

A few months later around my birthday, money was a little tight and I was waiting on a check to come in the mail. My mom went to the mailbox, and inside was a card for me from my ex. When I opened it, there was a check for $200, which was exactly the amount I was waiting for. Let me expose the enemy for a second. The check had the appearance of a blessing, but a gift connected to bondage is not a blessing at all. When my dad heard about it, he told me to rip up the check; his daughter could not be bought. I ripped up the check, and that same day, the money I was waiting on arrived, with no strings or chains attached.

I believe when we spend time in God's Word and in worship, He will not give us mess. Like me, you can pick up someone and try to stamp God's name on them, but that won't make them His gift to you. His Word says, *"No good thing will He withhold from those who walk uprightly before Him,"* (*Psalm 84:11*). A husband is a good thing. I believe that when we are nearing the season of marriage, God will begin to download characteristics and traits concerning our mate. He will give us information concerning the choice He has for us. He will not leave us ignorant. I now say, don't date until you know your mandate (your purpose and call). During this time I didn't know mine.

I remember dating another young man, and early on I asked if he had any children. I don't have a problem with children, but I want to know if I'll be possibly entering a blended family. I have a right to decide if this is something I want or not. Well, I was told no, and I didn't think anything of it. Then a few months later, he wanted to talk to me. He made it seem so serious that I thought something was wrong. He embraced me and then whispered, "I have a son." My initial reaction was accepting, but later that night, I was really bothered. If he could lie about having a child, what else had he lied about? When I would ask him if he had talked to his son, he always had excuses about how he and the child's mother didn't get along. Even if that were the case, it did not excuse him from making the effort needed to bond with his son. So I would give him suggestions, but he wouldn't follow through. Ultimately, I realized that I could not see myself with someone who was not too concerned about his own flesh and blood. How could he say he loved me, a person who he barely knew, but not love a child who he helped to create? It didn't make sense. So I chose not to continue the relationship. The decision didn't come without a struggle, but I decided not to allow my emotions to override my values.

As women we can be emotional. But even in our emotions, we need to look for truth. If our "love" for someone goes against everything we stand for and everything we believe in, how can that be real love? How can love contradict everything we are striving for? Shouldn't love compliment and add value? If love goes against our core values, then we will have division and no peace. Which is exactly the opposite of what love is supposed to do.

Before we venture into new relationships, we should evaluate some of the old ones. Were there signs you missed? Or did you see the signs and choose to ignore them? What stopped you from investigating the red flags? It takes a lot to walk away from a relationship, but we have to know that we are valuable and there are people who can see and appreciate that value. As for those who don't see or acknowledge our value, it is their loss not ours. It's hard enough dealing with deception in relationships, but even more devastating than being deceived by others is when we lie and deceive ourselves. When we deceive ourselves, we make it easy for others to manipulate us.

These deceptive relationships do not always involve strangers; sometimes they are with family. We do not choose which family we are born into. So many families have skeletons in their closets that can potentially destroy multiple households if exposed. Family deception truly takes time to be healed from. It takes a lot of effort to walk in forgiveness—but it can be done.

In the story of Rachel, we see how deceit and deception can cause us to develop sensitive skin. Rachel was loved by a man, but manipulated by her family. Family deception can cause deep wounds and ultimately give us sensitive skin.

Leah was tender eyed; but Rachel was beautiful and well favoured.

--Genesis 29:17

Sibling rivalry is the first and greatest battle of all time. We can assume there may have already been some tension between Leah and Rachel based on the physical descriptions given for them. One was called "tender-eyed," which means unattractive, while the other was called "beautiful." These were features neither woman had any control over, yet they clearly caused strife. We see this scenario played out over and over again. It can be based on hair texture, hair length, skin complexion, body shape or eye color. The list is endless, and it shows how factors outside of our control can cause division, jealousy and even hatred. Some are able to embrace differences, but others are not.

And Jacob loved Rachel; and said, I will serve thee seven years for Rachel thy younger daughter. And Laban said, It is better that I give her to thee, than that I should give her to another man: abide with me. And Jacob served seven years for Rachel; and they seemed unto him but a few days, for the love he had to her. And Jacob said unto Laban, Give me my wife, for my days are fulfilled, that I may go in unto her.

-- Genesis 29:18-21

This had to be an exciting time for Rachel. She had met a man who was willing to work to marry her. Jacob committed himself to her immediately by sacrificing seven years of hardship and labor for her. She had to be glowing everyday watching him work up a sweat, knowing all that effort was for her hand in marriage. And while other suitors may have been interested; Jacob was the one her father approved of.

And it came to pass in the evening, that he took Leah his daughter, and brought her to him; and he went in unto her. And Laban gave unto his daughter Leah Zilpah his maid for an handmaid. And it came to pass, that in the morning, behold, it was Leah: and he said to Laban, What is this thou hast done unto me? Did not I serve with thee for Rachel?

Wherefore then hast thou beguiled me?

--Genesis 29: 23-25

Can you imagine watching your dreams disappear in an instant? Jacob had done what was right and was tricked by Rachel's father. Rachel must have been devastated. Her hopes and dreams that had been built up over seven years vanished in one night. I'm sure this caused some bitterness and anger towards both her father and sister.

Unfortunately, some of us were born into unfair circumstances. Some of us had siblings who were favored more than us and caused deep wounds. Some of us were made promises, by parents and people we trusted, which were not kept. These situations wounded us deeply, and although many of us are now adults, the sensitivity remains.

And Laban said, It must not be so done in our country, to give the younger before the firstborn. Fulfil her week, and we will give thee this also for the service which thou shalt serve with me yet seven other years. And Jacob did so, and fulfilled her week: and he gave him Rachel his daughter to wife also. And Laban gave to Rachel his daughter Bilhah his handmaid to be her maid. And he went in also unto Rachel, and he loved also Rachel more than Leah, and served with him yet seven other years. And when the LORD saw that Leah was hated, he opened her womb: but Rachel was barren.

-- Genesis 29:26-31

Rachel is eventually given to Jacob as a wife. However, she is barren. The scripture does not state the cause of Rachel's barrenness but her emotional state could certainly have been a factor. When we have deep hurt, it can cause our potential to remain dormant. It is like a river that has been blocked by a boulder. The potential for it to flow is there, but the boulder must be moved out of the way first.

As the eldest sister, Leah was given to Jacob due to the custom of the day, so it was not really her fault. Even so, the ordeal must have caused Rachel significant tension, strain and stress. Sometimes we are used as pawns for someone else's gain. This will cause us to have ill feelings toward those who are using us as well as others who are also being used. We learn from Rachel these feelings of hurt can cause significant damage and possibly hinder our destiny. Many of us have had dreams and visions that we could not birth because of an emotional boulder. Many of us have destinies blocked by negative emotions.

And when Rachel saw that she bare Jacob no children, Rachel envied her sister; and said unto Jacob, Give me children, or else I die. And Jacob's anger was kindled against Rachel: and he said, Am I in God's stead, who hath withheld from thee the fruit of the womb?

--Genesis 30:1-2

Rachel's sensitive skin has ruptured. She attempts to blame Jacob for her dilemma, while envying her sister for having what she cannot. Envy is a very powerful emotion. Webster defines it as "painful or resentful awareness of an advantage enjoyed by another joined with a desire to possess the same advantage." Some synonyms for envy are covetousness, jealousy and resentment. When you open the door for one sin of the heart, many more will follow. You must deal with the root issue. You cannot blame others for what is on the inside of you. You must forgive.

I heard someone say, "Hurt people *hurt* people." When a person is hurting, they often lash out at those around them. Rachel was hurting and took out her frustration on Jacob. How many wives do this to their husbands, and vice versa? How many siblings do this to each other? How many co-workers do this to each other? Forgiveness is the way to heal your sensitive skin so that you can stop injuring those around you.

Leah has sons back-to-back. To cope with her jealousy, Rachel gives Jacob her handmaiden as her surrogate to have children. However, just like with Sarah and Abraham, the plan backfires. Everyone is able to have children except for Rachel. Leah birthed six sons and a daughter, and Rachel's maid had two sons. By this time, Rachel realizes that she has to approach the situation another way. She begins to heal her sensitive skin by getting into the position of prayer, most likely a pleading prayer. In her pleading she would have also asked for repentance.

22 Then God remembered Rachel; he listened to her and enabled her to conceive. 23 She became pregnant and gave birth to a son and said, "God has taken away my disgrace."

-- Genesis 30:22-23

When you get tired of seeing others participate in what you know you should be a partaker of, pray. When you get tired of your destiny being delayed, pray. When you get tired of seeing your dreams disappear, pray. When we earnestly pray from a repentant heart, the emotional boulder blocking our river will begin to move. Rachel is an example of sensitive skin that needed more toner—so she prayed.

Many of us have to face the ugly truth that some of our relationships – be they with family, friendships or romances – are birthed in deception. In reading Rachel's story, we see the emotional roller coaster deception introduces to relationships. But her story also confirms that there is hope even after great pain. With the Word as cleanser and prayer and repentance as toner, God can help heal the most broken skin.

Prayer

Father, I ask You to heal me from the wounds of my childhood. The self-inflicted wounds and those caused by family and friends. I take responsibility and repent for any wounds I have inflicted on others. Deliver me from all bitterness, anger and resentment. Help me to forgive those who have wounded, deceived or abused me. I want any emotional boulders that may be hindering my life to be removed. Help me to love in spite of the circumstances. I desire to be whole and complete.

Chapter 14
Tiffany's vs. Wal-Mart

We are all beautifully and wonderfully made in the image of God; born with gifts and talents for a purpose and a plan. We are valuable and unique, set apart and priceless. As women, the jewel of God's eye, we all start out in Tiffany's. At Tiffany's the collections are luxurious and first class in value. God views us in the same way— luxurious, first class, and valuable. The problem is some of us don't see *ourselves* that way. Some of us were deceived and left Tiffany's for Wal-Mart. We became impatient waiting around for someone to recognize our value. We did not want to wait for someone who could "afford" us. In haste, we moved from a place of luxury to a place of discount.

When I think of Wal-Mart, I think bargain, discount, cheap deals and inexpensive. I'm not saying the discount chain stocks poor quality, but there are some things that are more valuable when purchased elsewhere. For example, a ring from Tiffany's and a ring from Wal-Mart are two different kinds of rings. They have different qualities, characteristics and attributes. One has is highly valued, the other is of significantly lesser value. One is very exclusive, while the other is easily accessible. And it is the same way with us.

When we recognize that we are of Tiffany's quality, we will not accept just anything that comes our way. In actuality, certain people will not even approach us because they will already know that they can't "afford" us. Not that we're wearing a price tag but our character will indicate our value. Many people won't even go into Tiffany's because they know what the name represents and the price tag that goes along with it. Wal-Mart, however, is known for their low prices and bargains. As a woman, do you want to be known as high value or as a bargain steal? When you live a life that is pure and holy, it adds value to your character. The opposite holds true for a sinful life.

Some of us were in Tiffany's, but we were stolen or had to leave for reasons beyond our control. We were in the right place, but a thief came in and took our innocence. Some of us had just been placed in the display case when we were removed prematurely, and we do not remember the quality and value that the Jeweler—God, our Father—gave to us when He fashioned us. When placed in a new environment, some of us adapted to what we thought was right. We were taken so far away from our original place that it was hard for us to gain a sense of identity. However, there has always been something in us saying that there is more. We have been searching, trying to find the Tiffany store once again. We realized much of what we were told was lies, and we have been desperately trying to find our way back home. Let me encourage you, home is closer than you think.

Please understand that we can't expect Tiffany's quality from a Wal-Mart relationship. We cannot hang out at Wal-Mart expecting Tiffany's customers to find us. We cannot expect Tiffany's service while standing at a Wal-Mart counter.

The story of Naomi represents someone who was in Tiffany's, and due to issues beyond her control, ended up in Wal-Mart. Her new location effected, and eventually transformed, her skin type. From what we read, it does not appear that Naomi was always bitter, as her name means "my joy" or "pleasant." However, her life experiences caused her skin to turn dry.

In the days when the judges ruled, there was a famine in the land. So a man from Bethlehem in Judah, together with his wife and two sons, went to live for a while in the country of Moab. ² The man's name was Elimelek, his wife's name was Naomi, and the names of his two sons were Mahlon and Kilion. They were Ephrathites from Bethlehem, Judah. And they went to Moab and lived there.

-- Ruth 1:1-2

In reading these scriptures, we are unable to see what type of woman Naomi was, but we do learn something of note. Although there was a famine in the land, Bethlehem, the place of Naomi's people, was a place of blessing. When Naomi's husband moved the family, he left the place of blessing. Not only did he leave a blessed place, he settled in Moab, which was a place full of wickedness. The Moabites were known for their idol worship.

³ Now Elimelek, Naomi's husband, died, and she was left with her two sons.

-- Ruth 1:3

The cause of death for Naomi's husband is unknown, but the place of his death is significant. He died in a foreign land. He had taken Naomi away from everything she had ever known and now she was by herself, left alone to raise their sons. Based on her customs and upbringing, she probably could not marry a Moabite. This is a sad cycle, which many women fall into. We are lured away by the enemy, and then he leaves us open and vulnerable. We end up around people who do not really know us. One of the enemy's greatest traps is isolation.

130

⁴ They married Moabite women, one named Orpah and the other Ruth. After they had lived there about ten years, ⁵ both Mahlon and Kilion also died, and Naomi was left without her two sons and her husband.

-- Ruth 1:4-5

Although Naomi's sons could not replace her husband, I am sure they brought Naomi joy and comfort before they died. We don't know the time span of the deaths from one son to the next; nevertheless, she experienced three major tragedies in her life. Within ten years of her move, just as she is fully beginning to settle, she is deprived of her original family. Only God can heal this type of grief.

Many of us have experienced tragedy in our lives, some more than others. Perhaps you have had three significant situations that have brought you heartache. At this point Naomi does not talk about her emotions, but we know that she is hurting. When one is cut, in order for healing to take place, a scar develops over the wound. The problem is that some scars take a long time to heal, making an area that was once smooth, hardened.

⁶ When Naomi heard in Moab that the LORD had come to the aid of his people by providing food for them, she and her daughters-in-law prepared to return home from there.

-- Ruth 1:6

What's interesting is that we do not know when Naomi got the news that bread had returned to her homeland and the famine was over. The main point is that she heard the good news in a foreign land.

131

Likewise, God can visit us and give us direction in the Wal-Mart of our hardship.

⁷ With her two daughters-in-law she left the place where she had been living and set out on the road that would take them back to the land of Judah.⁸ Then Naomi said to her two daughters-in-law, "Go back, each of you, to your mother's home. May the LORD show you kindness, as you have shown kindness to your dead husbands and to me. ⁹ May the LORD grant that each of you will find rest in the home of another husband." Then she kissed them goodbye and they wept aloud.

-- Ruth 1:7-9

Upon hearing the good news Naomi decides to go home, to the place of relief. Many of us were born and raised in the church. We know the scriptures, songs and sermons, yet we still manage to get off course. Naomi's example demonstrates that even when we're off course, God's compassion never fails. We can always come home. This principle is further demonstrated through the kindness and love Naomi showed to her daughters-in-law. She could have commanded them to come with her, to leave everything they had known as she had for an uncertain future. But she showed compassion and allowed them to return to their homes. Many of us had people who were kind and dedicated to us during our time off course. There were people who ministered to us and loved us. We must be careful that we do not become so depressed that we don't abuse those who love and care for us. Naomi lost her husband and two sons. She was full of grief and had a long journey home. But, despite this she knew her daughters-in-law loved her, and did not take advantage of them.

Although Naomi's skin type was dry, there were still normal patches. She was able to retain some of her good qualities, which was indicated by her daughters' love. They did not want her to leave and lifted up their voices and wept when she did. Even in Naomi's sorrow, she did not want her daughters to suffer in an unfamiliar environment as she had. This is one of the few times we hear Naomi's words spoken with love. Her heartfelt blessing provides a great example for us to follow. Regardless of your situation, choose to speak life. In this instance we can see that Naomi's spiritual skin was cracked, but she still had some normal skin left.

[19] So the two women went on until they came to Bethlehem. When they arrived in Bethlehem, the whole town was stirred because of them, and the women exclaimed, "Can this be Naomi?"[20] "Don't call me Naomi," she told them. "Call me Mara, because the Almighty has made my life very bitter. [21] I went away full, but the LORD has brought me back empty. Why call me Naomi? The LORD has afflicted me; the Almighty has brought misfortune upon me."

-- Ruth 1:19-21

These verses give insight into Naomi's emotional state. She is hurt and bitter, but she made it home. In the previous verses she blessed others, yet spoke negatively about herself. Many of us can want well for others, while speaking negativity over our own lives. We can be our own worst enemy. It is important to pay attention to what we speak over ourselves. Some of us may act like we're just joking when we say something negative about our appearance or situation, but in actuality, it is just a mask for the pain and self-rejection we are inflicting on ourselves. This subtle trick is a lie from the enemy. Many people say, "I'm going to come to God when I get everything together." We have to be like Naomi and come home in whatever state we are in. The point is get back to God. He will take care of the rest.

One day Ruth's mother-in-law Naomi said to her, "My daughter, I must find a home for you, where you will be well provided for.

-- Ruth 3:1

After Naomi was settled back home, the love of God flowed through her. Her conversations changed and were no longer laced with bitterness. Once she returned to her rightful place, the wisdom of God brought provision for her. What doors will thrust open when we return to our rightful place? What wisdom will flow out of us when we step into our rightful place? What awaits us when we obey and return home?

[14] And the women said unto Naomi, Blessed be the LORD, which hath not left thee this day without a kinsman, that his name may be famous in Israel. [15] And he shall be unto thee a restorer of thy life, and a nourisher of thine old age: for thy daughter in law, which loveth thee, which is better to thee than seven sons, hath born him. [16] And Naomi took the child, and laid it in her bosom, and became nurse unto it.

-- Ruth 4:16

The same woman who declared that the Lord left her is now experiencing the miracle of nursing a child in her old age! Others even acknowledges God for using a relative to re-establish and restore life unto Naomi. The same woman who was bitter and dry is now has a new reason to live. Naomi's dry skin which had been healing since her return has now become normal.

We can learn so much from Naomi's story. We see how her life was blessed when she made it back to Tiffany's (her homeland). Naomi's Wal-Mart (Moab) experience brought immeasurable tragedy to her life. We may not have the same tragedies, but if we are in Wal-Mart, we are out of place. God, the Jeweler, is waiting to clean us, polish us, restore us and proudly place us back on display at Tiffany's if we are willing to make the choice to return home. A blue box awaits us. The choice is ours.

The Original

Before you looked in a mirror and began to critique, I saw you in My image as beautiful and unique.

Before you began to consider the opinions of men, I saw you strong and mighty one who didn't waiver or bend.

Before you listened to the words which others spoke over you, I saw you divinely gifted and powerful in all you do.

Before society tried to define who you are, I saw you as My jewel, My shining star.

Before you were hurt, misunderstood and confused, I saw you healed, whole and one of My divine tools.

Before you were I was and you were with Me, in spirit I saw you complete with an eternal destiny.

In the spirit I placed in you gifts of all kinds, I called you to be free not limited by space or time.

And now I call you back to the original of what I saw before, life tried to offer you a false hope and a false door.

I come to reveal, I come to unveil, I come to expose the strategies and plans of hell.

I show you his tactics, I teach you his ways, I uncover the traps and the snares he lays.

He is a defeated foe, he has been brought to light, I teach your hands to war and your fingers to fight.

I come to redeem, I come to restore, I come to bring joy, hope and so much more.

I Am the deliverer, I set the captives free, I liberate the soul and mind to have true liberty.

I loose the shackles, I break the chains, I take the burdens, I take the pains.

Just place it in My hands, just lay it at my feet, For I am the one your soul longs for and seeks.

I come to heal and bind up every wound, I hear your cry, I hear your prayers, I know your tune.

I come to bring you back to the place you first belonged, it will not be delayed, it will not be prolonged.

For I desire you to see you as I do, strong, gifted and powerful too.

Embrace this march to freedom and watch what I do, I bring you back to the original, the place of Me and you.

Chapter 15

Good Cry

There is a beauty with holiness. Holiness means to be set apart, consecrated and dedicated. Being holy helps make you pure physically and emotionally. I genuinely honor those who have kept themselves for marriage. Being a virgin, a sign of purity, is not promoted or celebrated in today's culture. But it is a blessing to allow yourself to be set apart (the actual definition of holy) for the man God has for you. If you are on that path, I honor you and implore you stay on it. Those who have been intimate prior to marriage can still be purified. Purification simply represents that you have allowed yourself to be cleansed and made whole. You can get back on the path and stay abstinent until marriage. I've personally been celibate for over a decade, so it can be done. There is a peace that comes with being sexually pure. God promises peace; the enemy only gives you frustration.

I went back and taught at the high school I graduated from. I started as a substitute then took over a class for a semester. While teaching there, I would tell my students, "You can ask me anything. I may not tell you everything, but what I do tell you will be the truth." Many of the students loved to see me standing at the door as their sub. We would talk about life and real issues. I remember a situation with one of the young ladies who was having some real challenging issues. At the suggestion of a fellow teacher, I was advised to speak with the young lady. When I subbed for her class earlier in the week, the topic of abortion came up. The young lady seemed very angry and vehement when she addressed the other students. Alerted by her demeanor, I invited the young lady to come speak with me after class.

I had her sit next to me, and I asked her what was wrong. She said she didn't think God loved her anymore. She went to church, but felt distant. She said she did something that God would never forgive her for. I told her there is nothing we can do that God will not forgive us for. I told her He loved her. The fact that we were having this conversation was Him showing her His love.

Then with watery eyes, she whispered that she'd had an abortion. I asked her if she repented. She said yes as her tears flowed. Then I stretched out my palms to her and began to catch her tears. I told her God loves you and He's wondering, "Where is my daughter? She used to talk to Me, she used to read My Word. I miss her. Where is my daughter?" The tears just flowed. I told her Jesus is catching these tears, and as they fall into my hands, they are falling into His. Not only does He catch them, He bottles them up. I told her she needed to have a good cry with God. We talked some more, then I hugged her and she left freed from the weight she came in with.

After that day, every time I saw her in the halls I'd ask, "Did you have that good cry yet?" For a few weeks her reply was no. About a month later, she came looking for me and was all aglow. She finally had her cry with God. He healed her and she knew she was forgiven.

There are many of us whom the enemy has lied to, telling us that what we have done is unforgivable, but he is a liar. All he wants to do is keep you in bondage. Jesus came to set you free. Not only does he desire to set you free but he desires that you be free indeed.

This is just one story of what a good cry can do. There are a myriad of issues that could bring us to have a good cry. Hannah is a biblical example of the power of a good cry. With Hannah we see how circumstances beyond our control can cause us to develop sensitive skin. Health concerns and outside forces can have a substantial effect on how we feel about ourselves. Sometimes, because of what we've gone through, or are going through, people might misunderstand us. It is okay to be misunderstood by people, as long as we know that we are always understood by God. Hannah exemplifies how our difficulties can push us to the place where we learn to change our skin type.

There was a certain man of Ramathaim-zophim, of the hill country of Ephraim, named Elkanah son of Jeroham, the son of Elihu, the son of Tohu, the son of Zuph, an Ephraimite. He had two wives, one named Hannah and the other named Peninnah. Peninnah had children, but Hannah had none.

--1 Samuel :1-2

So we clearly see the issue here. In those days having children was an honor. It was a blessing for a woman to birth and nurture children; barrenness was considered a curse. So naturally the main desire of women of the time was to have children (the more the merrier). It brought great shame to them if they did not have any. Hannah might have been okay if she were the only one married to Elkanah. But, unfortunately, he had another wife who was able to conceive. This reflected poorly on Hannah because now it was obvious to everyone that the problem did not fall on her husband, it was her. Oftentimes it's easier to deal with an issue when we believe that we are not the cause of it, but when we find out that we are, it makes us very sensitive.

And this man went up out of his city yearly to worship and to sacrifice

139

unto the LORD of hosts in Shiloh. And the two sons of Eli, Hophni and Phinehas, the priests of the LORD, were there. And when the time was that Elkanah offered, he gave to Peninnah his wife, and to all her sons and her daughters, portions: But unto Hannah he gave a worthy portion; for he loved Hannah: but the LORD had shut up her womb. And her adversary also provoked her sore, for to make her fret, because the LORD had shut up her womb.

--1 Samuel 1:3-6

In this account we see that Elkanah's love for Hannah was strong despite her inability to conceive. He did not see children as a prerequisite for his love. There are many of us who have people in our lives that love and care about us, but because we feel inadequate in some area, we cannot fully accept their love. Have you ever seen someone who seems to have everything, yet they are still unhappy? Have you ever known someone live a life others wish they had, and they feel they are still missing something? Elkanah gave Hannah a double portion of honor in their marriage, but it could not remove the pain of being childless. External rewards can be helpful, but they will not fill every void in our lives.

Not only was Hannah battling internally, she also had to cope with being taunted by Peninnah, her husband's other wife. It's awful when you have an issue and someone is there picking on you and belittling you about it. Peninnah was doing to Hannah what the devil does to us. When we are at a low point, he comes to nag, insult and irritate us. He uses people to do this. Many times during a rough situation, he will send people to say some of the most hurtful things. The enemy loves to see you low, and he wants you to stay that way. As we proceed, you will see this as a place you can overcome, and rise above.

So it was year after year; whenever Hannah went up to the Lord's house, Peninnah provoked her, so she wept and did not eat. Then Elkanah her husband said to her, Hannah, why do you cry? And why do you not eat? And why are you grieving? Am I not more to you than ten sons?

--1 Samuel 1:7-8

Hannah's issue did not last three months or six months; it persisted for years. Is there a situation in your life that has been going on for a long time? Any long-term irritation or difficulty will cause pain and discomfort. Peninnah was right there, constantly reminding Hannah of her inadequacies. Have you ever known someone who knew your heart's desire and decided to achieve it for themself, and then flaunted it in your face? That's just evil.

You may have a good husband who works and provides for you and the children. You want for nothing, yet you are still unhappy. There might be a void that you have been carrying all of these years. It's not that you don't appreciate your husband; there is simply a place that only God can fill for you so you can be complete. This may be a revelation to some of you. The void may be that dream you always wanted to pursue, that business, book or charity foundation. Although everything around you seems perfect, there is still something missing, and it has been nagging at you for years.

So Hannah rose up after they had eaten in Shiloh, and after they had drunk. Now Eli the priest sat upon a seat by a post of the temple of the

LORD. And she was in bitterness of soul, and prayed unto the LORD, and wept sore. And she vowed a vow, and said, O LORD of hosts, if thou wilt indeed look on the affliction of thine handmaid, and remember me, and not forget thine handmaid, but wilt give unto thine handmaid a man child, then I will give him unto the LORD all the days of his life, and there shall no razor come upon his head.

--1 Samuel 1:9-11

You have to get to the point where enough is enough. Hannah arose and went to the House of the Lord. It does not say Hannah talked to people or went with a group; she took her problem straight to God. Hannah poured all of her hurt and distresses out to God. In times of severe distress we can be moved to come to God and pray like we have never prayed before. Life's issues can cause us to pull something out of ourselves that we didn't know was there. Hannah did not care what she looked like when she came to God. She had an unresolved issue that she had been battling with long enough. She was at the end of her rope with nothing else to lose.

Hannah came to God and humbly asked Him to look upon her situation, vowing to give back to Him what she desperately desired for herself. She was specific in what she asked for, and by saying a razor would not touch his head, she indicated that the child would be consecrated or "set apart" for God (holy). Many of us have tried every way possible to fulfill our dreams. We used every contact and connection to no avail. But we must be like Hannah. We must submit that dream, business, book—or whatever the desire—to God. And don't just submit

142

it, vow to also consecrate it to Him. Vow that it will be pure and set apart. Whatever you submit, like Hannah, make sure it will be holy.

And as she continued praying before the Lord, Eli noticed her mouth. Hannah was speaking in her heart; only her lips moved but her voice was not heard. So Eli thought she was drunk. Eli said to her, How long will you be intoxicated? Put wine away from you. But Hannah answered, No, my lord, I am a woman of a sorrowful spirit. I have drunk neither wine nor strong drink, but I was pouring out my soul before the Lord. Regard not your handmaid as a wicked woman; for out of my great complaint and bitter provocation I have been speaking.

-- 1 Samuel 1:12-16

Everyone isn't going to understand your dream or vision. Everyone isn't going to understand your passion or desire. Do not be offended if you are misunderstood. Many of us miss out because we get offended when those around us can't see or won't support our vision and we become bitter. Our dreams are not for everyone to understand. When we are preparing for greatness, we may look crazy to other people, even to people we love and respect the most. But sincerity can bridge that gap. Honesty and dedication can communicate for us.

Then Eli said, Go in peace, and may the God of Israel grant your petition which you have asked of Him. Hannah said, Let your handmaid find grace in your sight. So [she] went her way and ate, her countenance no longer sad.

--1 Samuel 1:17-18

143

Although Eli perceived wrong and misunderstood Hannah, he still blessed her. Her response toward him could have been negative, but she remained humble, and in doing so, she allowed Eli the opportunity to speak blessings over her life. When she received the Word, her countenance changed. The Word healed her and she went from sensitive to normal skin in an instant. When we are humble in the presence of God, no matter what our skin type is, immediate changes will take place.

Hannah became pregnant and in due time bore a son and named him Samuel [heard of God], Because, she said, I have asked him of the Lord.

--1 Samuel 1:20

Hannah received her promise, and we can also. Hannah's internal and external issues pushed her to a place of no return. Forced her to cry out for her destiny and promise. Many of our issues are actually pushing us toward our destiny and our promise. The path may not be comfortable, but that does not mean the blessing is not on its way. We don't know if Hannah would have been as desperate if she had been in a more comfortable situation. Some of our difficult times are a set up for transitions and breakthroughs. Hannah is an example of how prayer and faith can heal sensitive skin and make it normal.

Hannah had her good cry before the Lord about the deepest and most painful desire of her heart. Have you had your good cry yet? What will await you when you get in that place and pour out your soul? What weight will be lifted? What promises will be renewed? What passions will be ignited? What dreams will come true? Cast your burdens on the Lord, and have a good cry.

Prayer

Father, I thank you that I can come to You with anything. I lay every hurt, care and worry at Your feet. I will no longer carry the burdens of guilt, shame and condemnation. I receive Your forgiveness and Your love. Fortify my character to not be offended when I'm not understood. Help guard my heart from rejection and fear. I thank you that Your plans for me are good and not of evil, to bring me to an expected end. I willingly give You my hopes and desires like Hannah and commit to them being sanctified and holy. I desire for them to bring You glory. Forgive me for when I've tried to accomplish them in my own strength. In this season I truly surrender and yield to Your leading and guiding.

Recap of The Bible Figures

Samaritan Woman at the Well

Skin type: Oily

Regimen applied: Honesty

Esther

Skin Type: Normal

Regimen applied: Obedience, Humility, Wisdom and worship

Abigail

Skin Type: Combination

Regimen applied: Wisdom, Humility

Ruth

Skin Type: Normal

Regimen: Loyalty, Good Work Ethic, Faithfulness, Humility

Sarah

Skin Type: Combination

Regimen: Obedience, Faith

Lot's Wife

Skin type: Dry

Regimen: None/Death

Mary Magdalene

Skin type: Oily

Regimen: Praise and Worship, Humility, Boldness

Rachel

Skin type: Sensitive

Regimen: Prayer, Repentance

Naomi

Skin type: Dry

Regimen: Ability to hear and respond, Wisdom

Hannah

Skin type: Sensitive

Regimen: Earnest prayer, Humility, Consecration, Faith

Final Touches

"Beauty of Holiness"

You were formed for a purpose and with a plan,

You were created by His divine hand,

You were fashioned in His image and His light,

His shining through your life makes it beautiful and bright.

You bring pleasure with your words and your smile,

Your wisdom shared with other keeps you on their speed dial.

Your fruit is desired by all who are blessed to see,

The love, joy, peace and integrity that grows from your tree.

Your holy dimensions shine like cut diamonds and light up a room,

Allowing your very presence to break darkness and gloom.

You've been purified and cleansed through the fires of trial and tribulation,

Molding a soul, once good, now spotless in His salvation.

You carry His attributes, His likeness and speech,

Giving your words His power and soul-searching reach.

You are humble and gracious, merciful and kind,

Genuine and honest, peaceful and patient, of His design.

His glory surrounds you and draws people near,

They approach you with ease, an inviting spirit they shall not fear.

As you walk into destiny you make His name glorious,

You are a queen, a jewel, the Beauty of Holiness.

Give unto the LORD the glory due unto his name: bring an offering, and come before him: worship the LORD in the beauty of holiness.

I pray the words in this book have brought healing, clarity, understanding and empowerment. It is my hope that this book led you on a journey full of highs and lows, bumps and turns, and has now placed you at the beginning of a rewarding path.

Life is a series of trial and error. Some of us have tried multiple brands and types of skincare products in both our natural and spiritual lives. We have tried different natural application techniques and products. Spiritually, we have tried different religions and belief systems. Find the skincare brand that works for you then share it with others.

I have found the skincare brand that works perfectly for me. That brand is Jesus Christ. It's been rated number one by spiritual beauty advisors for over 2,000 years. His skin regimen will cleanse, tone, moisturize and exfoliate. No one can wash away our sins like Jesus. No other regimen provides a proper skincare balance like Jesus. No one can exfoliate our past and our present and continually cleanse like Jesus. Won't you try Him today?

The fact that you are reading this book means that you are willing to invest in you. Yet, a monetary sacrifice alone is not sufficient. A lifestyle change is necessary. For every dollar spent beautifying the outside, we should spend one minute working on the inside. As a makeup artist I have watched women spend over $700 on makeup to beautify themselves externally. What awesome, radiating beauty would result from spending 700 minutes on our internal adornment?

149

I was born and raised in the church, but strayed when I grew older and got off course. In 2001, I made the final decision to follow Jesus. I fell in love with Him and my life has been changed ever since. I've had trials and successes, suffered lows and gloried in the highs. Through it all I've learned to praise God. I've been what I call, "saved for REAL" for over a decade. I've committed my body, mind, will and my all to Him.

Living holy and pure before God has been such a joy. I've experienced a level of love that I did not know existed. Even the loss of friends along the way and being misunderstood has been a blessing as it helped me to grow in grace. Before embarking on this journey, I often felt insecure about myself both internally and externally. For over ten years, God has been purging, purifying and perfecting me. I have spent time studying and reading the Bible incessantly, allowing the Word to work in me and through me. He is my joy, my peace and the lover of my soul. My journey with Him has brought me more joy and peace than I could have asked for or imagined. I consistently love Him more today than I did yesterday.

Some of you may be curious as to how this book came about. After observing the changes I made to my lifestyle over the years, my cousin Katina (Garrison) Jones called me in 2009 and asked me to speak at her church, not as a speaker within a group, but as the sole speaker. I was shocked and excited. She gave me the theme: "The Beauty of Holiness." I instantly knew it was the perfect vehicle to parallel the skills I learned as a makeup artist with the spiritual concepts God had given me to share. After delivering the message, I sensed something larger had taken place. In preparing for the sermon, I had gathered so much information, and I realized I wouldn't be able to share everything. Stepping off of that podium, I knew that I was stepping into my destiny and into what God called me to do. I took the notes and research before God and allowed Him to add the increase. You are reading the baby produced from that labor of love. My prayer is that something written on these pages will spark, ignite and motivate you to become who God created you to be.

Just as a gardener prepares for planting season by making sure he has all the right tools, I pray that what you have read will give you the tools you need and that the seeds of knowledge have fallen on good ground. As you continue to nourish this new understanding, I pray that its roots will grow deep down so that you will begin to flourish. In time the seed will sprout the fruit of the Spirit, which will blossom and bloom and become a beauty of holiness that others can bask in and benefit from throughout your life.

CLEANSING Prayer:

Father, in the name of Jesus, I repent for everything against Your will for my life. I ask You to wash me and cleanse my internal skin. Father, create in me a clean heart and renew a right spirit within me. I renounce all unholy thoughts, people, habits and ways. Father, search me and reveal to me all that is displeasing to You. I release all bitterness, hurt, shame, vengeance, anger, hatred, lust, evil-thinking, fear, pride and guilt. Father, I pray for deliverance in every area of my life. I renounce the sins of _____. Father, forgive me. Today I commit myself to You. I believe that Jesus came, died and rose again for me and I accept him into my heart today. I humble myself to Your teaching, leading and guidance. I thank You for the plan You have for my life. I thank You for your mercy and Your grace. I thank You for healing and restoring me. I commit myself totally to You. In Jesus' name, Amen.

TONING Prayer

Father, I pray that You increase my hunger and thirst to seek you. May my prayer life increase. My I be a witness of answered prayers and petitions before You. Teach me how to pray with accuracy and humility. Cause me to pray not only for myself but for others. Let me be sensitive in my prayer time to pray for what is in heaven to be done on earth. I thank you that You hear me and that my prayers do not fall to the ground or on deaf ears. Let me have such an excitement in prayer as I commune with You. Cause me to be open to hear Your voice and let us dialogue together. I thank You that nothing is too hard for You, and when I come to You, the answers are provided. Cause my prayer life to grow by leaps and bounds. In Jesus name, Amen.

MOISTURIZING Prayer

Let my worship be pure before You. Inhabit the praises of my lips oh God. Let the words of my mouth and the meditations of heart be acceptable and found pleasing in Your sight. Let my worship be from a sincere and deep place. May the praises of Your goodness be forever on my lips. I will worship and praise You for your faithfulness, Your holiness, Your sovereignty. You are great and greatly to be praised. I thank You for the love that You show me continually. You've been so good, I can't stop praising You. May a song forever be in my heart for You. In Jesus name, Amen.

EXFOLIATION Prayer

As I yield my body to You, let my fasting cause bonds to be broken and for me and others to experience freedom. Let my fasting cause me to increase in my hunger and desire for Your word and Your presence. I desire You more than my necessary food. Let my body be submitted to Your leading and guidance. Let my fasting cause me to walk in greater levels of obedience and trust. Let my fasting yield fruit that shall remain. In Jesus name, Amen

Your beauty should not come from outward adornment.... Instead, it should be that of your inner self, the unfading beauty of a gentle and quiet spirit, which is of great worth in God's sight.

--1 Peter 3:3-4

Natural and Spiritual Essential Ingredients

Now in the natural there are many types of products to accommodate the different types of skin. But regardless of skin type, you want a product that will maintain your skin's natural oils, not strip them while still removing any impurities, makeup and dirt. The same in the spirit, there are many scriptures you can study and meditate on to help maintain your spiritual core. Your spirit's current skin type and situation will determine the types of scriptures (i.e. ingredients) you need to look for. Here are a few natural ingredients[19] to consider...

Oily Skin

- ☐ Lemon - This oil is known for its astringent and anti-irritant qualities. It balances overactive sebaceous glands that lead to oily, blemished skin, clearing and enlivening the complexion.

- ☐ Peppermint - Is used to cleanse and tone. It purifies sluggish skin and pores and is suitable for use on oily skin, acne and blackheads. Is useful for minor skin irritation and inflammation.

- ☐ Lime (distilled) - Astringent, antiseptic and non-irritating. This oil is useful in the treatment of acne.

154

- Grapefruit - Uplifting, cleansing and clearing. This oil is stimulating to the lymphatic system and toning to the skin.

- Willow Bark - This extract contains natural beta hydroxy acids, which work as a natural skin exfoliant to help unplug follicles and pores.

- Evening Primrose - Helps soothe acne prone skin resulting in clear and healthy looking skin.

- Cedarwood, Geranium, Clary, Lavender, Ylang-ylang, Niaouli, Cajeput, Cypress, Frankincense, Patchouli, Roman & German Chamos, Sandalwood, Juniper, Melisa, Coriander, Rose, Rosemary, Eucalyptus, Red Mandarine, Myrtle, Neroli

Dry Skin

- Almond - Helps replenish skin oils lost during the cleansing process, while producing a gentle massaging effect during exfoliation.

- Carrot Seed - Valued for its soothing, relaxing properties. It is believed to stimulate cell renewal as well as the sweat and sebaceous glands. It is beneficial to mature or dry skin, helping to deter or reduce wrinkles. It also protects skin exposed to weather extremes.

- Wheat Germ - This oil is very high in vitamins, particularly Vitamin E, carotene, and lecithin. Its high Vitamin E content acts as an antioxidant and preservative

- Cedar Wood - For its calming, purifying properties and is used to benefit the skin and tissues near the surface of the skin

- Sandlewood- It is also used as an astringent, which helps in tightening the skin, giving it a fresh look.

- Clary, Jasmine, Geranium, Lavender, Orange, Palma Rose, Neroli, Castor, Extra Virgin, Rosewood, Rose, Vetiver, Ylang-ylang: these oils are great for oily skin

Combination Skin

- Geranium - The oil is highly therapeutic, antiseptic and an astringent. It can help users relax and cope with pain. It also brings a radiant glow to skin.

- Rose - This oil has soothing and gentle cleansing properties that have a softening and refining effect on skin. It is an antiseptic and mildly astringent for dry or chapped skin, helping to restore pH balance, and is excellent for use on all skin types.

- Neroli - The oil is thought to increase circulation and stimulate new cell growth. It can help prevent scarring and stretch marks, as well as calm, soothe and normalize the skin.

- Rosewood, Ylang-ylang, Hydrosol

Sensitive Skin

- Carrot Seed Oil - This thin, yellow oil distilled from ground seeds is rich in beta-carotene and is valued for its soothing and relaxing properties.

- Yarrow - Is valued for its cleansing, toning, anti-inflammatory and healing properties. It also encourages blood flow to the skin.

- Roman & German Chamomile, Rose, Palma Rosa, Helichrysum, Neroli, Rosewood, Angelica, Jasmine: these oils are great for sensitive skin

Normal Skin

- Atlas cedarwood, almond, orange, palmarosa, roman, chamo, rosewood, Ylang-ylang,

- Geranium - The oil is highly therapeutic, antiseptic and an astringent and can help users relax and cope with pain. It also brings a radiant glow to skin.

157

- Jasmine - This oil helps to soothe and moisturize

- Lavender - An excellent, all-purpose skin care oil thought to have antiseptic, antibacterial and antiviral properties, as well as cytophylactic properties that promote healing and help prevent scarring

- Soy - This oil is high in linoleic and oleic essential fatty acids and vitamin E. Soybean oil exhibits excellent emollience, helps with cell renewal and improves skin's appearance and health.

- Neroli - The oil is thought to increase circulation and stimulate new cell growth. It can help prevent scarring and stretch marks, as well as calm, soothe and normalize the skin.

- Evening Primrose - Is exceptionally high in essential fatty acids, which condition and restore moisture to the skin.

- Rose - This oil has soothing, gentle cleansing properties that have a softening and refining effect on skin. It is antiseptic and mildly astringent for dry or chapped skin, helping to restore pH balance, and is excellent for use on all skin types.

- Tea Tree - The oil is best known for its antiviral, antibacterial and antifungal properties. It can help to fight all three categories of infectious organisms (bacteria, fungi and viruses). For skin and hair, Tea tree has been used to combat acne, oily skin, head lice and dandruff.

- [ ] Atlas Cedarwood, Almond, Orange, Palmarosa, Roman, Chamo, Rosewood, Ylang-ylang,

Here are some essential spiritual ingredients:

All Skin Types

- [ ] Psalm 51:10 - Create in me a clean heart, O God; and renew a right spirit within me.

- [ ] James 2:20b - Faith without works is dead?

- [ ] Proverbs 3:5-6 - Trust in the LORD with all thine heart; and lean not unto thine own understanding. In all thy ways acknowledge him, and he shall direct thy paths.

- [ ] Philippians 2:5 - Let this mind be in you, which was also in Christ Jesus.

- [ ] Matthew 6:33 - But seek ye first the kingdom of God, and his righteousness; and all these things shall be added unto you.

- [ ] Psalm 51:17 - The sacrifices of God are a broken spirit: a broken and a contrite heart, O God, thou wilt not despise.

- Romans 12:1 - I beseech you therefore, brethren, by the mercies of God, that ye present your bodies a living sacrifice, holy, acceptable unto God, which is your reasonable service.

Oily Skin Essentials

- John 3:16 - For God so loved the world, that he gave his only begotten Son, that whosoever believeth in him should not perish, but have everlasting life.

- 1 Corinthians 15:33 - Be not deceived: evil communications corrupt good manners.

- Amos 3:3 - Can two walk together, except they be agreed?

- James 4:7 - Submit yourselves therefore to God. Resist the devil, and he will flee from you.

- 2 Corinthians 6:17 - Wherefore come out from among them, and be ye separate, saith the Lord, and touch not the unclean thing; and I will receive you.

Dry Skin Essentials

- Hebrews 3:15 - While it is said, Today if ye will hear his voice, harden not your hearts, as in the provocation.

☐ Ephesians 4:31 - Let all bitterness, and wrath, and anger, and clamour, and evil speaking, be put away from you, with all malice.

☐ Hebrews 10:22 - Let us draw near with a true heart in full assurance of faith, having our hearts sprinkled from an evil conscience, and our bodies washed with pure water.

☐ Proverbs 17:22 - A merry heart doeth good like a medicine: but a broken spirit drieth the bones.

Combination Skin Essentials

☐ Psalm 41:4 - I said, LORD, be merciful unto me: heal my soul; for I have sinned against thee.

☐ Philippians 4:8 - Finally, brethren, whatsoever things are true, whatsoever things are honest, whatsoever things are just, whatsoever things are pure, whatsoever things are lovely, whatsoever things are of good report; if there be any virtue, and if there be any praise, think on these things.

☐ Psalm 51:6 - Behold, thou desirest truth in the inward parts: and in the hidden part thou shalt make me to know wisdom.

Sensitive Skin Essentials

- ☐ 1 Peter 2:2 - As newborn babes, desire the sincere milk of the Word, that ye may grow thereby.

- ☐ Proverbs 16:24 - Pleasant words are as an honeycomb, sweet to the soul, and health to the bones.

- ☐ Psalm 51:7 - Purify me with hyssop, and I shall be clean [ceremonially]; wash me, and I shall [in reality] be whiter than snow.

- ☐ Psalm 34:18 - The LORD is nigh unto them that are of a broken heart; and saveth such as be of a contrite spirit.

Normal Skin Essentials

- ☐ Ephesians 5:15 - See then that ye walk circumspectly, not as fools, but as wise.

- ☐ 2 Timothy 1:6 - Wherefore I put thee in remembrance that thou stir up the gift of God, which is in thee by the putting on of my hands.

- ☐ 3 John 1:2 - Beloved, I wish above all things that thou mayest prosper and be in health, even as thy soul prospereth.

- [ ] Philippians 2:5 - Let this mind be in you, which was also in Christ Jesus

About the Author

MaShani Allen, the "Golden Scribe" challenges women to discover and redefine their self-image. As a make-up artist, model and fashionista, MaShani's experience and expertise in the entertainment industry enables her to illuminate both the internal and external issues underlying difficult times of transition and uncertainty.

"Many have asked me for external beauty tips but deeply desired to know truth and discover how to grow in God. That is the most pressing area of concern because it's where True Beauty is found..."

An upstanding empowerment speaker, teacher and confidence coach, MaShani received her undergraduate degree in Advertising from the University of Florida, and masters degree in Christian Counseling from Word Bible College.

Her "Goduate" certification was earned through instruction and training at Crusaders Ministries, Chicago IL (under Apostle John Eckhardt), and has been applied at Regency Christian Center, Whittier, CA (under Apostle Jason and Pastor Cathy Guerrero) where she is an established leader and founder of the Regency Kingdom Training Program, a platform that utilizes teaching, training and activation to empower and equip believers of Jesus Christ to fulfill God's purpose.

Through various speaking engagements, specifically the Free to Live conference, Lifebuilders Conference and Lifebuilders seminars, MaShani has been given the opportunity to impart wisdom, affirmation and

164

strength into many lives. The speaking platform has evolved and expanded, most recently into a weekly Periscope teachings where host MaShani Allen delves deeper into the beauty of holiness, "scoptifying" her audience with an emphasis on inner beauty, character development, and the foundational beauty attributes least often considered in our externally-focused lives.

"So many look for Beauty on the outside and are unaware that True Beauty starts from within."

A native of Miami, Florida, MaShani's love for the beauty industry began as a teenager and continues today. It is through this passion that she has been blessed to empower women of all ages, nations and walks of life to enhance their God-given beauty, both inside and out. The international reach of her ministry has been a continuously inspiring and humbling experience for her and is evidence of Matthew 6:33 at work in her life.

MaShani Allen's beauty resounds from the inside and out, and runs Spirit deep. Her chief desire and purpose is to share that beauty with you.

Please utilize the links below to connect with MaShani and begin your beauty journey today.

• Social media @MaShaniAllen (LinkedIn, Periscope, Facebook, Twitter, Instagram, YouTube).
• Request information for teaching, training, speaking, and conference sessions on her website at:

www.MaShaniAllen.com

Notes

All poetry in this book are original works by MaShani E. Allen unless specifically credited otherwise.

1. Derrick, Julyne. What Type of Skin Do You Have?

http://beauty.about.com/od/skinflaws/a/skintypes.htm

2. Adkins, Jen. Characteristics of Combination Skin.

http://skincare.about.com/od/skin101/a/comboskin.htm

3. Your Fitness Guides: "Skin care" (analysis), Health-Cares.net, 2007.

http://skin-care.health-cares.net/oily-skin-care.php

4, 5, 6, 7. Derrick, Julyne What Type of Skin Do You Have?

http://beauty.about.com/od/skinflaws/a/skintypes.htm

8. Derrick, Julyne. 4 Basic Skin Care Needs: The right (& wrong) ways to cleanse, moisturize & exfoliate your skin.

http://beauty.about.com/od/skinflaws/a/basicskincare.htm

9. Slick, Matt. What is Prayer? Christian Apologetics & Research Ministry.

http://www.carm.org/christianity/prayer-ministry/what-prayer

10. Baker Books, The Complete Works of E.M. Bounds on Prayer 1990, p.5

11. Baker Books, The Complete Works of E.M. Bounds on Prayer 1990, p.17

12. St. John Providence Health System, Faith and Health: Faith Community Partnership Letter. (Jan – Feb 2012)

https://www.stjohnprovidence.org/upload/docs/Community%20Health/JanFeb_FaithHealth.pdf

13, 14, 15, 16. Sykes, Clay The Reality of Spiritual Seasons.

http://www.lighthouseprophecy.com/prophecy/TheRealityofSpiritualSeasons.html

17. Adkins Jen. What Causes Acne - Our Top 5 Acne Myths Might Surprise You. http://skincare.about.com/od/oilyskin/tp/Top-5-Acne-Myths.htm

18. Common Skin Cake Mistakes. http://www.beauty-advices.com/common-skin-care-mistakes

19. Burt's Bees, Ingredients Glossary. https://www.burtsbees.ca/c/shop/ingredient-glossary.html

Organic Facts, List of Essential Oils.

http://www.organicfacts.net/organic-oils/natural-essential-oils/list-of-essential-oils.html

International Wellness Directory, Essential Oils: Their Properties.

http://www.mnwelldir.org/docs/therapies/essentia02.htm

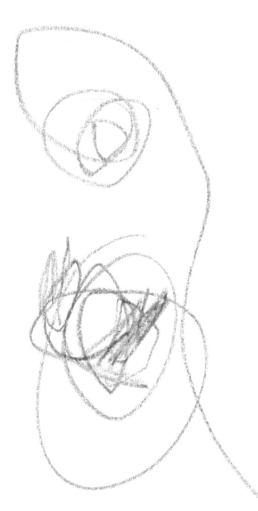

CPSIA information can be obtained
at www.ICGtesting.com
Printed in the USA
LVOW13s1916050517

533412LV00010B/676/P